LITTLE ANNIE OAKLEY

and Other

RUGGED PEOPLE

Little Annie Oakley

& Other

Rugged People

BY STEWART H. HOLBROOK

THE MACMILLAN COMPANY · NEW YORK

1948

For WILLIAM M. DOERFLINGER

who suggested it

Author's Note

OVER a period of years almost any American writer will have developed an interest and often an enthusiasm for a wide variety of things native to his country. Ours is a big country, too, yet big as it is, I never cease to marvel at the incredible number of places, people, and events, both past and present, that I should like to write about. But were I to have the lives of four men, placed beginning to end, I could scarce accomplish the object.

In the past twenty years and more, however, I have many times come upon subjects which for one reason or another were so compelling as to cause me to lay aside whatever book I was working on and devote—gladly enough—my time to them. They appeared in magazine or newspaper articles, commonly referred to among the higher literati as fugitive pieces.

Then, one day, came a friend, William Doerflinger, to suggest that a modest portion of the book-reading public might enjoy a collection of my fugitives between hard covers. The editors of the periodicals concerned were without exception both prompt and graceful in granting permission to use the pieces in book form; and I thank the men of the *American Mercury*, the *American Scholar*, the *New Yorker*, the *New York Times*, the *Saturday Review of Literature*, *Life*, *Esquire*, and the *Country Press*.

Portland, Oregon   STEWART H. HOLBROOK

Contents

LITTLE ANNIE OAKLEY

and Other

RUGGED PEOPLE

*She could shoot the head off
a running quail, could*

Little Annie Oakley

WHEN she was almost nine, little Phoebe Mozee took down the enormous cap-and-ball rifle that hung over the cabin fireplace, and went out into the surrounding woods where she blew the tiny head clean off a running quail. The remains of that bird should have been stuffed and sent to the Smithsonian Institution, for it had served as the first target of the future Annie Oakley, "Little Sure Shot," the world's greatest markswoman and the sweetheart of generations of American males. Annie died in 1926, pretty much forgotten. Twenty-two years later she again became one of the greatest personalities in show business. As the heroine of *Annie Get Your Gun* (portrayed by Ethel Merman), which celebrated its second anniversary still going strong, she was the toast of Broadway. Although Broadway's "Annie" has better lines, the real Annie had a life no librettist could improve on.

Annie Oakley unquestionably was wonderful. She stood quite alone in her celebrity, which cannot be likened to that of any currently famous female. Her flavor was unique and of her time. It was a sort of combination of Lillian Russell and Buffalo Bill, a merger of dainty feminine charm and lead bullets, the whole draped in gorgeous yellow buckskins and topped with a halo of powder-blue smoke.

The phenomenon was born Phoebe Anne Oakley Mozee, in 1860, in the backwoods of Darke County, Ohio, the sixth of eight children of Jake Mozee and his wife Susanne, both Quakers. Jake died from exposure in a blizzard when Annie was four. Her mother remarried and the new home was a pretty dismal place. Her stepfather was not much of a provider. That there was always food on the table was due largely to little Phoebe's uncanny and natural ability with a muzzle-loader. And presently, when she learned that hotels in Cincinnati would pay actual cash for quail and rabbits, she became a market-hunter.

Shooting matches were the favorite sporting events of the time and place. Darke County, Ohio, like all other back-country regions, could muster any number of expert riflemen. One after the other, and to their considerable chagrin, the little Mozee girl mowed them down. A professional named Frank Butler swaggered into Cincinnati and challenged anyone in those parts to shoot for $100 a side. The Mozee girl took him on.

Little is known about the match except that live birds were used and so were shotguns—a weapon the Mozee youngster held fit only for little children—and that the girl won the match. She also shot an arrow straight into the heart of Frank Butler. Mr. Butler married her and they went on the road as a shooting act. It wasn't long before the girl, who now dropped the Phoebe and became Annie Oakley, was the featured part of the act.

In the spring of 1885, the team of Butler and Oakley signed on with Buffalo Bill's Original Wild West Show, just getting into its full stride under the able management of Nate Salsbury and the inspired press-agentry of Major John W. Burke, without question the mogul of all press agents. No honest account of Annie Oakley, or for that matter of Buffalo Bill, can be written without reference to Major Burke.

Burke would be wholly incredible today. He wore his hair long and occasionally called himself Arizona John. He hailed from that suburb of Arizona we know as the District of Columbia where he was born and reared. He had been a tramp newspaper man and once was manager of a trained-animal act. Dressed impressively in a Prince Albert and striped pants, he wore his whiskers in the prominent banker or flying buttress style and his sole interest was that Buffalo Bill's Original Wild West Show should become and remain the most gigantic, the most stupendous and the most amazing spectacle on the face of the earth.

Fifteen years before, a journalist called Ned Buntline had taken hold of William F. Cody when Cody was an obscure cavalry scout and had blown him into the magnificent character of Buffalo Bill, Prince of the Plains. When Buntline and Cody parted company Burke got a firm grasp on the Buffalo Bill legend and built it into even greater stature, built it so solidly, too, that no reliable biography of Cody has been or ever will be written. And now, in 1885, Major Burke took little Annie Oakley by the hand.

Among Burke's many talents was a gift for getting along with American Indians. The best-known Indian villain of the day was the surly yet bighearted old Sioux medicine man, Sitting Bull. Burke and Salsbury inveigled him into joining the Buffalo Bill show, and presently the press of the country broke out with a wonderful story, namely, that Sitting Bull, whose name was still a terror to all palefaces, had joined the show simply to be near his adopted daughter, who was none other than Annie Oakley. Moreover, swore Burke (and newspapers printed every word of it as gospel), Sitting Bull had made Annie a "full Indian princess" and named her "Watanya Cicilia"—which, so Burke related with awe, meant Little Sure Shot.

Although, just as in the case of Bill Cody, Major Burke dreamed up the character that Annie Oakley became, her shooting itself needed no ballyhoo. It was as near perfect as shooting could be. At thirty paces she would slice the thin edge of a playing card held by Frank Butler. She exploded cartridges thrown into the air. While she sighted by looking into a mirror formed by the glittering blade of a long bowie knife, she broke a ball whirled around Butler's head. She was pretty good with a six-gun, too, and one of her favorite stunts was to roll a tin can along the ground with a tattoo of bullets from a pair of Mr. Colt's double-action revolvers.

Great days were ahead for Annie. The show went abroad, first to England, where it set up at Earl's Court in London. After a run of middling to poor business the gate picked up. Lady Randolph Churchill engaged a box. So did the Messrs. Gilbert and Sullivan. So did Sir Charles Wyndham, the noted actor. And presently, on a wonderful day that Major Burke never permitted the world to forget, the Prince of Wales (the future Edward VII), his princess and their three daughters, together with other assorted royalty, came for a special performance. By heroic measures Burke managed to keep Buffalo Bill, one of our really great topers, sufficiently sober to appear on his white horse and break a few glass balls with his rifle. The yelling Indians, the careening Deadwood coach, the bandits, all proved exciting to these princelings, whom Burke insisted on calling "crowned heads," but it was Little Sure Shot they had come to see. Next day Buffalo Bill received a note: "Sir; Will the little girl, Annie Oakley, who shoots so cleverly in your show, object to shooting a friendly match with the Grand Duke Michael of Russia? We will arrive at Earl's Court at 10:30 this morning." It was signed "Edward."

Bill Cody was upset. He believed, and with reason, that no matter how good a marksman the grand duke was, little Annie would shoot rings around him. And, when asked, Annie said that was exactly what she would do. Buffalo Bill thought it would be quite terrible to have a grand duke outshot by a commoner and a woman at that. Annie was not to be moved. While the argument was going on, four whole carriage loads of assorted royalty and nobility rolled up to Earl's Court and the shooting match started. The duke was a better-than-good marksman but not in Annie's class. He missed fifteen out of fifty targets, Annie only three.

The incomparable Major Burke announced to reporters and cabled back to the U.S. that the grand duke had really come to England to win a British princess in marriage and had even progressed to the engagement stage, but that his losing the shooting match to a woman had caused him also to lose face. Hence the engagement was broken by the princess. "How magnificent this little woman of the Great Plains!" marveled Burke. "She and her magic gun won *two* matches from the grand duke—the shooting trophy and the hand of the princess." Even Annie Oakley came to believe it.

The sporty Prince of Wales liked the Wild West Show. He came again and again, and near the end of its run he presented a fine medal to Miss Oakley. And at last Queen Victoria could stand it no longer. She commanded a special performance, while Major Burke's long whiskers fluttered as never before. It was all the same to Miss Oakley. Her eye unfogged by royalty, her hand still true, she stood out there in the arena and broke ball after ball, punctured card after card, then bowed and retired gracefully in a cloud of smoke.

Whether Annie's success had made her too big for her pants or whether, as more likely, too many members of the show simply felt they were being ignored is not known. Whatever the reason Buffalo Bill and his crew sailed home without Mr. and Mrs. Butler. The Butlers went to Berlin where Annie gave exhibitions and later toured Germany. Then they returned to America, though not to the Original Wild West Show. Annie got mixed up with a stage show entitled *Deadwood Dick*, one of the most dreadful turkeys ever seen. A tour of vaudeville was not much better. What Annie needed was the inspired touch of Major John Burke.

In 1889 the Butlers were back with the Wild West Show. They toured France, Spain and Germany. In Berlin, at the special request of the young Kaiser Wilhelm, Annie shot the ashes off a cigaret held in his mouth. Two years later she was a sensation at the Chicago World's Fair, and for the next seven years she did not miss a season nor a single performance with Buffalo Bill. Then, in 1901, as the train carrying the show was steaming south to go into winter quarters, it ran head-on into another train. Four performers were killed and almost one hundred injured, among them Annie Oakley, who was pulled unconscious from the wreck by her husband.

Partial paralysis and five operations followed the injury. Annie's hair grayed, then whitened. It was more than two years before she took gun in hand again. Then she found she could still shoot and shoot well. Soon she was out with another stage horror, *The Western Girl.* She left it and went into vaudeville. The rest of her life was spent in and out of vaudeville and, during the winters, in giving lessons in shooting at Pinehurst, N.C.

Annie died in Greenville, Ohio, in her native Darke County, on November 3, 1926, and her body was cremated in Cincinnati. Childless herself, she left eighteen orphan girls whom she had befriended and put through school. Frank Butler died a few weeks later. Both Bill Cody and Major Burke were long since in their graves.

Until *Annie Get Your Gun* the new generation knew Annie Oakley only as a slang term for complimentary tickets. It was coined by the late Ban Johnson, the baseball impresario, who referred to baseball game passes, all of which were punched as though by bullets to distinguish them from paid tickets, as Annie Oakleys.

It was small immortality for so wonderful a woman. All young men of the time, and old men too, lost their hearts to the tiny buckskinned sprite and never quite got over it. No American male of the era was wholly immune to the charms of Little Sure Shot, adopted daughter of Sitting Bull and the creation of Major John W. Burke, God rest his inspired and imaginative soul.

Naked and alone in the great
woods was Joe Knowles,

The Original Nature Man

ON SULTRY July 20, 1914, newspapers
up and down the Pacific Coast announced in blaring headlines:
EYES OF WORLD ON TEST OF MAN VS. NATURE. Reading on, Western he-men learned that Joe Knowles, the Nature Man of Maine,
was about to plunge, unarmed and naked as a snake, into the un-
tamed, cougar-infested wilds of the Siskiyou Mountains of Oregon.

Next day, the *Examiner* of San Francisco, sponsor of this
one-man scientific expedition, gave over a goodly part of its front
page to telling who Joe Knowles was, what he proposed to do,
and the conditions of this test of Man vs. Nature. The *Oregonian*
of Portland did likewise, and lesser papers of the Coast region
broke out with syndicated articles signed by Knowles at his jump-
ing-off place, Grants Pass.

To assure the public there was no fakery, the *Examiner* announced it had secured two eminent naturalists as special in-
vestigators. They were Dr. Charles Lincoln Edwards, B.S., Ph.D.,
head of the Nature Study Department of the Los Angeles school
system, and Prof. T. T. Waterman of the University of California. The two savants would be turned loose in the same wild
district where Knowles was to perform and there circulate at
will, picking up messages that the Nature Man might write and
leave at agreed points. Also they were to set down their own im-

pressions of the experiment and generally act as "guardians of the public interest" in the affair.

Two days later the story was still front-page stuff and getting bigger and better all the time. Wearing a breechclout and nothing else, with no implement of any kind, Joe Knowles had shaken hands with professors and reporters, posed for Mr. Hearst's cameraman, and vanished into the Siskiyou jungle. There he was to remain for sixty days, unarmed, unaided in any way, living on nuts and berries, or on game if he could snare it with his bare hands; clothing himself as he could from the forest; and pitting his naked body against the enemies of nature, which ranged all the way from clouds of vicious insects to mean mountain lions. WILD BEASTS ROAR INVITATION TO JOE KNOWLES bellowed the *Examiner* in a banner, and there were echoes all the way from Los Angeles to Seattle.

There hadn't been such a local story since the San Francisco "Fire," and it was going great guns as July crept into its last week. Joe was doing well and sitting pretty, he reported in messages written in charcoal on bark and left for the two professors to pick up. He was living on fish and small game, taken in primitive fashion, and he was about to snare a deer from whose skin he would make himself more durable clothes than those he was wearing. Red-blooded he-men, with whom the West Coast has ever been infested, could scarcely wait for their morning papers to read—pop-eyed and envious—what the Nature Man of Maine had done the day before. It even got into the comic strips and editorial cartoons.

Then came that sinister 28th of July, when all Europe started blowing up. AUSTRIA DECLARES WAR ON SERBIA screamed headlines from coast to coast and on around the world. Twelve hours later the Russian mobilization was under way, and the Kaiser had declared war on the Czar. France rose to arms. On August 2, Germany demanded free passage through Belgium. Next day, von Kluck's Big Berthas were bombarding Liége. And on August 4, Great Britain went whole hog into the riot.

It was a sad day for Joe Knowles. And you can guess what it did to the *Examiner's* great experiment of Man vs. Nature. The Naked Thoreau news from Grants Pass went into the back pages next to the classified ads, and many a Californian doesn't know to this day whether Joe Knowles *ever* got out of the woods.

Joe was annoyed, and with considerable reason. What a lousy time to start a world war! Here he was, exposing his hide to the gnats and cougars, fighting a single-handed battle against all the natural enemies of Man—and Europe had to go and blow him off the front page. . . .

II

This, however, wasn't the first time that Joe Knowles had ventured alone into the primeval forest to prove that atavism is not only easy and pleasant, but good for newspaper circulation as well; nor was it his last trip of the kind. It was simply the one when all the breaks were against him.

The time that Joe really knocked them out of their seats was in 1913, a year before the Siskiyou affair. The setting was the woods of Northern Maine, the paper was the Boston *Post*, and the public included almost all the newspaper readers in New England and Eastern Canada. The story was handled with beautiful showmanship. When Joe went into the Maine woods in August, 1913, he was an unknown artist, a struggling portrait painter. Two months later he was a national figure, known alike to adults and schoolboys, and the center of a controversy that was second in noise only to that between the friends of Admiral Peary and the friends of Dr. Cook.

His Big Idea came out of a dream. "Not much of a dream," Joe said, "but a damned real one. I dreamt I was lost in the woods, alone and *naked,* with no hope ever of getting out. When I woke up I got to thinking if and how a civilized man should get along in such a situation. A day or so later I related my dream at a small hotel dinner. How a New York newspaperman happened to be present I have forgotten, but there was one; and next day the *Tribune* carried an interview with me, telling of my claims. In a day or two mail started flooding me."

The correspondence started a train of thought in Joe's mind. Some of the letters agreed that a naked and unarmed man could survive in the forest. Others said Joe was a fool who didn't know what he was talking about. And then, almost simultaneously, came letters from the Boston *American,* a Hearst paper, and the Boston *Post.* Both said they would like to have Joe call on them when he was in Boston. . . . The Big Idea was a-dawning.

First off, but in greatest secrecy lest the Vermonters have him clapped into jail on disorderly conduct charges, Joe conducted an undress rehearsal. Naked except for a G-string, and taking nothing with him, he went into the wooded hills back of Bradford and remained there a week. It was July. Berries were plentiful. So were flies and mosquitoes. But the dawning Nature Man rubbed his hide with wild spearmint and the pests passed him by. He cornered trout in a small pool and caught them with his hands. Fire was easy, for Joe had learned the secret years before from Indians. All in all, he put in a pleasant and interesting week. When he emerged from the Bradford woods he packed his grip and went to Boston.

For reasons not at all clear today, the editor of the Boston *American* hemmed and hawed. "You're losing the chance of a lifetime," Joe told him as he walked out, and how true he spoke any Boston newspaperman will tell you now.

So Joe went over to the *Post.* Even in 1913, the *Post* was an old paper, but it wasn't doing well. The loud *American,* still young and rowdy, was giving New England a sample of Hearst at his best, or worst, and it had seemed to Knowles that the Hearst sheet was the logical medium for his experiment. At the moribund *Post*, however, Joe found a real welcome. Charles E. L. Wingate, late general manager of the Boston *Journal*, had just taken hold of the Sunday edition, and he was open to new ideas. He also had some of his own. And so, late in July, Editor Wingate wheeled up his heavy guns and fired a double-truck barrage that startled the natives as they hadn't been startled since Paul Revere rode through Middlesex.

A man, a naked man, a man used to all the comforts of civilization, was about to plunge into the Maine wilderness to learn whether the human race had become so sissified that it could no longer combat the rigors and dangers which beset Primitive Man. It was a highly dangerous test, the *Post* took pains to point out, for fierce animals stalked silently through the forest lanes, and there was ever the specter of starvation.

But Joe Knowles was a fine physical specimen. Harvard College said so. Called in by the *Post*, Dr. Dudley Allen Sargent, physical director of the university, looked Joe over carefully and told the world:

Sandow was perfect in strength and development. Knowles is perfect in strength and development. Further, Knowles has probably the staying power of three Sandows.

Now all was in readiness for the great test. The *Post* thoughtfully invited newspapers of other cities to the remote point in Maine where the Nature Man was to take off. The New York *Sun* thought well enough of the story to send its ace feature writer, Frank Ward O'Malley; and there were a score of lesser lights from various dailies. On August 4, 1913, Joe bid them all good-by and walked into the silence of the Dead River country, attired only in a breechclout.

For the next sixty-one days, New England, New York, and

other parts of the country served by the *Post's* special syndica-
tion, were agog at the swellest feature story in a generation. It
was Steve Brodie, Nellie Bly, and Stanley-and-Livingstone all
rolled into one great juicy series. The reporters wrote their heads
off, and every day or so they would come across a birchbark
message, left in a forked sapling by the Nature Man; Joe had
been living on roots and berries—he had caught and cooked
some fine trout—he had made rude sandals of bark—he was
digging a pit in which to catch a bear—he had caught a bear
and was enjoying bear steak—he had got some hemlock bark
and was tanning the bear's skin—he would soon have a robe—
he had caught a deer with his hands, and he was now wearing
hide moccasins.

At this, the game wardens of towns round about let out a howl.
It was agin' the law to kill deer out of season, gun or no gun,
and they were a-goin' to take this crazy man into custody. The
wardens hoisted their badges and rifles and struck into the
woods to arrest the Nature Man—and newspaper circulation
soared again. Tipped off about the wardens by his contact man,
Joe headed northward and crossed the Canadian border late in
September.

The Canucks left him alone. Free once more from the harass-
ments of civilization, Joe turned out some neat sketches in charcoal which the *Post* reproduced for a public that couldn't get
enough of its Nature Man. Circulation had jumped by now to
400,000 copies, or about double the normal figure.

The nights were getting chilly up in Quebec, Joe reported via
birchbark, but he was sleeping warm in his bearskin robe. Time
was beginning to hang heavy on his hands, too, for reporters
came across a painting—not a sketch—that Joe had made, using
the juice of roots and berries for his colors and a well-chewed
twig for a brush. Of course, there weren't messages from him
every day, but his terse dispatches were so expertly timed and

spaced that they kept the newspaper reading public on edge. The *Post's* circulation mounted to 436,585, and there must have been a deal of groaning over in the offices of the Boston *American.*

III

On October 10, Joe emerged from the woods at Megantic, Quebec. He was the picture of health, rugged, tanned, and bearded; and he was met, you may be sure, by a small army of newspapermen, both Canadian and American. Even a movie outfit was present.

"My only regret at the time," Joe recalled in telling of it, "is that I didn't manage to catch a cub bear alive. I thought it would be a fine idea to come out of the woods leading a small and tamed bear behind me on a leash of willow."

Escorted to Boston on a special train, Joe was distinctly the man of the hour. Big shots of Boston flocked to the Copley-Plaza for a banquet tendered the Nature Man. Newsreel men dogged his steps, while low comedians at the Old Howard staged a Kno Jowles burlesque. Vaudeville booking agents from New York fought to offer a contract, and a janitor swept out Tremont Temple for Joe's first lecture before highbrows. But now, amidst the big whoopee, crept in that sour and envious note that so often attends success in any form. The *American* told its readers that on the morrow it would bring forth a "complete exposé" of the Nature Man. Its announcement hinted at gigantic skulduggery on the part of Knowles and the *Post,* and it promised shocking revelations.

The *Post* had got wind of the coming blast even before it was announced. It also got a court injunction prohibiting the *American* from publishing a story which it held was a gross libel. Things happened rapidly in the *American* office, once the injunction was served. The story was already out, in the early bulldog edition, and men were sent forth to bring in all copies of this edition. The front page was broken up, the exposé story killed, and there was no mention of Joe in the regular city edition. That is, no mention except for a striking full-page advertisement announcing publication of *"Alone in the Wilderness,* by Joe Knowles, the Nature Man." It was neatly timed: the book sold more than 300,000 copies.

The *American* said nothing more about Knowles. It didn't even mention a suit for $50,000 which Joe had brought against the paper for printing the "slanderous story" in the early edition, copies of which had pretty well permeated New England outside of Boston. But, in any event, a magnificent controversy had been loosed. Was it true, as an investigating reporter of the *American* had averred, that the Nature Man had spent most of two months lolling around in a deserted but comfortable logging camp? Had Joe been living like a backwoods potentate, attended by innumerable stooges in the form of guides, hunters, and bull cooks? Was it so that no less than four small holes, suspiciously like bullet holes, had appeared in the bear robe? Had a leather expert of Boston vowed that the little deerskin had been tanned by a commercial process? And was young Billy Lavaway lying when he told a backcounty Maine paper that he had been sent out of the woods by Joe to get some cigarets; and that when the kid had returned with Piedmonts, Joe had angrily roared he had ordered Sweet Caps? Did the *American,* in short, have it right when it termed Joe Knowles the "Doc Cook of the Maine Woods"?

Those were fighting words in those days, and Joe and the *Post* fought back. They fought with heavy ammunition in the shape of affidavits of Maine guides, opinions of nationally known naturalists, and of at least one United States senator. Joe took the platform in Boston's Tremont Temple and challenged his detractors to come forward. They came not, but the thing had become a *cause célèbre* and New England was in turmoil. It was great for circulation, too.

With the booming of charges and countercharges ringing in his ears, Joe took to the Keith Vaudeville Circuit for twenty weeks with 24-sheet billing and $1,200 a week.

IV

Knowles later declared that because of the "exposé" incident, seven employees of the *American* were fired. In any case, the hatchet was buried, for *Hearst's International*, a slick-paper monthly magazine, came out with an editorial, done in brisbanal style, paying high compliments to Joe:

We thank Knowles for his experiment. It is a noble piece of poetry. A naked man against the tooth and claw of Nature, and coming out victor —clothed, fed, healthy; it is a deal more comforting to our proper human pride than the erection of a Woolworth building.

Less than a year later, Joe took into the wild Siskiyous for Hearst's *Examiner* of San Francisco, as related. Despite the unseasonable breaking out of the World War, Mr. Hearst had seen what a Nature Man could do for circulation, if but given a chance. So he had Joe go to New York, and there, in the summer of 1916, the *Journal* prepared to make up for what its sister paper in Boston had muffed.

This time the stunt was to be—appropriately enough, considering the sponsor—a double-barreled affair. There would be a Dawn Man, *and* a Dawn Woman, both of them naked and both of them out in the Great Silence, but *not* together. (Remember, this was in 1916.) The general routine was to be about the same as that used by Joe in his Maine and Oregon-California adventures. It was also announced that Knowles would give the Dawn Woman a week of serious woodcraft instruction before she went out on her own.

The Dawn Woman soon appeared, in the columns of the palpitating *Journal,* in the form of Elaine Hammerstein, said by the *Journal* to be "the beautiful society leader and well-known actress." Joe, of course, knew he was to play second fiddle in this experiment.

The country selected for the Dawn Woman's commune with Nature was the timbered region near Old Forge, in Essex County, New York, and the "special investigator" for the newspaper was no less than the eminent Dr. Woods Hutchinson. Joe took Elaine in tow (her mother was along as chaperon) and for a week or so he gave her intensive instruction in firemaking, weaving and fishing without tackle; and he showed her edible herbs, roots and berries native to the country. As Joe told it afterward, Elaine's enthusiasm for a Dawn life seemed perceptibly to lessen day by day during the instruction period.

But Elaine told the reporters that she was Ready and would Conquer. Boozy cameramen shot the pretty girl in all sorts of semi-Dawn attire; and they also snapped Joe in all his Cro-Magnon nakedness.

And then, on a blistering Sunday, the *Journal* double-trucked a spread that would make editors of today's tabloids sit up in envy. KNOWLES HURLS DEFY AT GRIM NATURE, said one banner; while another, somewhat leeringly, told how DAWN GIRL SLIPS NAKED INTO DARK FOREST. Young men decided to take up woodcraft. Goatish old males simply drooled.

The Dawn Woman lasted long enough to send out a few pathetic notes on birchbark. "Tango teas, Broadway, and matinees are a far cry from the absolute silence of the great woods," she wrote. At the end of seven days she came out of the absolute silence, and undoubtedly returned to her swell Riverside Drive home of which the reporters had made so much. "She just couldn't take it," was Joe's only comment.

With the Dawn Woman back in her sissy boudoir, there wasn't

any use sticking around, so Joe came out of the woods himself
and put on his pants.

V

For twenty years Joe Knowles made his home at Seaview on
a remote shore of the Washington coast.* The wild Pacific
breakers pounded his dooryard and high tides surrounded his
studio, where he painted and did etchings. At the age of sixty-
nine he was hearty and jovial. He held no animosity toward
those who sought to "expose" him, not even the guy who called
him the "Doc Cook of the Maine Woods." But he made it em-
phatically clear that he would not answer letters or other queries
about his Back-to-Nature experiments.

"I'm still sorry I didn't manage to catch a bear cub, up there
in Maine," he said wistfully. "It would have been a knockout—
parading out of that timber a-leading a bear like a Scottie. It's
just about the only regret I have. . . . That and that goddam
war breaking out when it did."

* Joe died there October 21, 1942, in the strange house he had put together, at
odd times over two decades, of the flotsam of and from wrecked ships. Outside the
gate, the last time I was there, still hung the sign "Stranger, Pause a While, Joe
Knowles."

I*t happened only once in three hundred years—*

Murder at Harvard

NOT all of the sons of Harvard, not even Harvard doctors of philosophy, appear to know that the university on the Charles was the scene of one of the most celebrated crimes in American annals. This is a melancholy state of affairs, for the setting of the murder was indubitably a college building and the criminal, who was John White Webster, A.B. 1811, and M.D. 1815, remains the only Harvard professor to perform lethally while a member of the faculty, and the sole college professor to gain entrance to the *Dictionary of American Biography* on the strength not of his scholarship but of his stout and murderous right arm.

The painful celebrity that came to Harvard has gradually been dissipated in the ninety-nine years intervening, yet more than one member of the faculty long felt the blight cast by Professor Webster. Bliss Perry has related how his mother at Williamstown, Massachusetts, refused to entertain a Harvard professor who had come there, circa 1870, as a delegate to a convention of New England college officials. Mrs. Perry vowed most firmly on this occasion that she could not sleep "if one of those Harvard professors was in the house." Incidentally, the professor, who had to find quarters elsewhere than in the Perry home, was James Russell Lowell.

One reason the crime achieved such notoriety was pungently pointed out at the time by the eminent Jared Sparks. "Our professors," said the then president of Harvard College, "do not often commit murder." Another reason for notoriety was the prominence of the victim, Dr. George Parkman. And witnesses at the trial read like the index to one of Mr. Van Wyck Brooks's charming studies of New England.

But let us move upon the *corpus delicti*.

II

At about half past one on the gray twenty-third of November, in 1849, Dr. George Parkman, one of Boston's best-known citizens, was seen afoot near the corner of Blossom and North Grove Streets, moving rapidly toward Harvard Medical School, on the Boston side of the Charles. He was always in a hurry, Dr. Parkman, and his tall, lean figure, together with a prognathous jaw and a set of false teeth so white they fairly glittered, made him a marked man. Yet somewhere near or at the entrance to the medical college he walked straight into Valhalla. Nor has he been seen since.

A man of Dr. Parkman's standing could not disappear without being missed immediately. It was he, a Harvard man himself, who had given the very land on which the then new Medical School building stood. He had also endowed the Parkman Chair of Anatomy, currently occupied by Dr. Oliver Wendell Holmes. His family was prominent, and his brother, the Rev. Francis Parkman, was a well-known clergyman whose son of the same name was about to achieve fame as a historian. The Parkmans were in-laws of many old Boston families, including that of Robert Gould Shaw.

When Dr. Parkman did not return to his home on Walnut Street that afternoon of the twenty-third, search was begun at once by Charles M. Kingsley, the agent who looked after Parkman's many properties in the city. And next day, Robert Gould

Shaw himself, after conferring with the Parkmans, had 28,000 handbills distributed announcing a reward of $3,000 for recovery of the doctor alive, or $1,000 for his body. Mr. Shaw told police that he suspected a man who several months previously had robbed Dr. Parkman.

While police were looking for this unnamed thug, an astonishing event occurred. On Sunday, two days after the doctor's disappearance, there appeared at the door of the Rev. Francis Parkman's home Professor John White Webster, who acted in "an abrupt and peculiar manner." Webster said that he had had an interview (a tremendous understatement, that) with the missing man in the Medical School on Friday afternoon, at which time he had paid Dr. Parkman $483 "and some cents." The latter had then, said Webster, rushed out of the college. All of which favored the popular theory that Parkman had been waylaid, robbed, and doubtless murdered.

John White Webster was fifty-six years of age. After graduation from Harvard Medical School he had served in Guy's Hospital, London, and married Harriet Hickling, a daughter of the American vice-consul at St. Michael. Since 1824, he had taught chemistry at Harvard, and from 1827 had held the Erving Chair of Chemistry and Mineralogy. The Websters, who had four lovely daughters, lived in Cambridge and were much given to hospitality.

Hospitality of the sort the generous Websters lavished on faculty members and wives, as well as local and visiting celebrities, cost a good deal, even in the Cambridge of a century ago. And Professor Webster's salary of $1,200 a year was not equal to it. True, he had the income from his lectures; but he was far from brilliant on the platform, and the income from this source was meager. Yet, while it was known to Robert Gould Shaw that on November 23 his brother-in-law had gone to collect money owed him by Webster, he did not suspect that Webster was responsible

for Parkman's disappearance. Who, indeed, *could* suspect any
such indiscretion in a faculty member of the college on the
Charles?

It was a fact, though, that the financial affairs of Professor
Webster had reached something of a climax. They were so in-
volved that many whole pages of finely printed testimony were
required, a bit later, to make them clear—if ever they did become clear—to the jury. Briefly, it would appear that as early
as 1842 Webster had first borrowed money from Parkman, in
the sum of $400. For this he gave his note secured by personal
property. Then, in 1847, at a time when the first loan had not
been repaid, Parkman had been one of a group to lend Webster
more than $2,000, this time taking a mortgage on all of his per-
sonal property, which included a cabinet of minerals. A year
later, unknown to Parkman, Webster went to Robert Gould Shaw
and by pathetic tales of misfortune prevailed on that kindly man
to buy the cabinet of minerals outright for $1,200. He failed to
mention that this collection was already in pawn to Parkman.

Well, it was bound to happen soon or late, and one day the
matter of Professor Webster's cabinet of minerals—soon to be
the most famous collection in history—occurred in a conversation between Gould and Parkman. Now, Doctor Parkman patently enjoyed a low boiling point, and he became furious. From
that moment onward poor Professor Webster knew what it was
like to have a Yankee bloodhound on his trail. His creditor was a
punctilious man who paid his own obligations when due and he
expected the same of everybody else, even a Harvard professor.

III

Nothing came of the search for Doctor Parkman. The Charles
was dragged. The Medical School was visited by swarms of police who also entered all of the college buildings in Cambridge.

Strangers in Boston were picked up by the score, to be questioned and released. The theory of robbery and murder still held the fancy of both police and public, and apparently nobody suspected Professor Webster until a morose and obscure man named Ephraim Littlefield began to translate his brooding into action. Littlefield was janitor at the Medical School. He must have been of a particularly suspicious nature, for his entrance into the case as an amateur detective was brought about by a generous act of Professor Webster's. On the Tuesday following Parkman's disappearance, Webster had presented Littlefield with a thumping big turkey—an outstanding event, since it was the first gift the janitor had received in seven years of work at the college. Littlefield brooded over the turkey, which one is happy to note came from Foster's store, next door to the Howard Atheneum, which a bit later became the place where generations of Harvard undergraduates were to study anatomy. Littlefield not only brooded over the gift of the turkey, but he was troubled because talk on the street had it that "they'll sure find Doctor Parkman's body somewhere in the Medical School." (In those days medical colleges, both abroad and at home, were held to be notorious receivers of the products of professional body-snatchers.)

"I got tired," said Littlefield in explaining his next move, "of hearing all that talk about the Medical School." Accordingly, he procured what appears to have been a sufficient number of demolition tools to have supplied wreckers for all of Harvard University. Into his dismal basement apartment at the Medical School he lugged drills, hammers, chisels, crowbars. He told his wife that he was going to do nothing less than to dig through the brick vault under Professor Webster's room in the college. Mrs. Littlefield was dreadfully frightened. She objected that her husband would be dismissed from his job, should knowledge of his suspicions reach officials of the college. But she apparently felt differently about the matter after her husband related a conversation he had overheard between Webster and Parkman.

A few days before Parkman's disappearance, according to Littlefield, the janitor was helping Webster putter around his laboratory. The two men were busy and didn't hear a footstep. But suddenly, as if from nowhere, Doctor Parkman appeared on cat's feet. Immediately, said Littlefield, Doctor Parkman spoke up quick and loud—and harsh: "Doctor Webster, are you ready for me. tonight?" And Webster replied: "No, Doctor, I am not ready tonight." Parkman moved back toward the door, raised one arm and shook one fist. "Doctor Webster," he said savagely, "something must be accomplished tomorrow." Then he went out.

For the next several days Littlefield brooded and wondered whether, on the next call Doctor Parkman made on Professor Webster, the latter had been ready for him. So, on what must have been a gloomy and foreboding Thanksgiving Day, and while Mrs. Littlefield stood watch for possible interruptions, the janitor hammered and drilled and crowbarred his way into the solid brick wall of the vault beneath Professor Webster's laboratory. Progress was slow. At noon Littlefield refreshed himself with the astounding turkey, then returned to his labors, which were great. They really laid brick walls to stay, in that era of solid craftsmanship, and night found the janitor only part way through the bricks. He was a determined man, however, and on the following day, after performing his regular duties, he resumed his attack on the vault. And that night he broke through. "I held my light forward," he related, "and the first thing I saw was the pelvis of a man and two parts of a leg. I knew," he added darkly, "this was no place for such things."

Nor was it. Littlefield notified the police of his find, and when they had taken one look at the ghastly contents of the vault, they drove madly to Cambridge in a hack and called on Professor Webster. Constable Derastus Clapp, a man of devious Yankee

ways, told Webster they should like him to attend them at the
Medical School while a new search was being made. Webster
replied that although the building already had been searched a
number of times, nevertheless he would be glad to accompany
the officers. He got into the hack, which soon crossed the bridge
into Boston—and continued on past North Grove Street and
toward Leverett Street Jail.

"Stop," cried Webster. "We are going in the wrong direction."

But devious Constable Derastus Clapp answered: "Oh, that's
all right, Professor. He is a new coachman and somewhat green,
but he will doubtless discover and correct his mistake." Boston
had constables in those days of Transcendentalism.

In a few moments, however, the professor realized that he was
not a free aid in a search, but a prisoner in Boston jail. Reporters
came, and next day the press and all the town went delirious.
"Horrible Suspicions!!" screamed the usually seemly and gen-
teel *Evening Transcript*, "Arrest of Professor J. W. Webster."
And it continued:

> Since last evening our whole population has been in a state of the
> greatest possible excitement in consequence of the astounding rumor
> that the body of Dr. Parkman has been discovered and that Dr. John W.
> Webster, professor of chemistry at the Medical School of Harvard Col-
> lege, and a gentleman connected by marriage with some of our most
> distinguished families, has been arrested and imprisoned, on suspicion
> of being the murderer. . . . Never in the annals of crime in Massa-
> chusetts has such a sensation been produced.

And then, because Epes Sargent was editor of the *Transcript*,
and because he probably wrote the story himself, we get the full
flavor of the *Evening Transcript's* idea of reporting the crime of
the century. The item continues:

> In the streets, in the market-place, at every turn, men greet each
> other with pale, eager looks, and the inquiry, "Can it be true?" And
> then the terrible reply, "The circumstances begin to gather weight

against him," is wrung forth; the agitated listener can only vent his sickening sense of horror, in some such expression as that of Hamlet—
O, horrible! O, horrible! most horrible!

Never again, so far as I am aware, did the *Transcript* feel that a murder called for Shakespeare. Not even the famous Richardson and Pretty Choir Singer affair of later years rated the Bard.

IV

The trial opened on the 19th of March, 1850, when Professor Webster, "his step light and elastic, crossed and took his seat in the dock, his countenance betraying a degree of calm and dignified composure." He was quite short in stature, and seemed of no great strength to "the expert stenographer," John A. French, who noted and took down everything for publication in a "splendidly illustrated" pamphlet put out by the Boston Herald Steam Press. I cherish a worn copy of this horribly printed pamphlet, and had a distant forebear of mine not been otherwise so tremendously occupied, family folklore might have added considerably to my knowledge of the trial. Peter B. Brigham was excused from jury duty at the Webster trial on the improbable plea that he belonged to the Boston militia, was "liable to call at any moment," and was "thus exempt by the statute from serving on a jury."

The State promptly put Janitor Littlefield on the stand, and his accumulated testimony was bad indeed for Professor Webster. Defense attempted to throw suspicion on Littlefield himself, and it also presented a long and highly distinguished array of character and other witnesses. The Hon. John Gorham Palfrey, historian, former editor of the *North American Review,* and member of Congress, declared sonorously that Professor Webster was a man of some temper but of extremely good heart. President Jared Sparks of Harvard thought Webster "kind and humane." Nathaniel Bowditch, probably a son of the great mathematician, said that Webster was "irritable though kind-hearted." Other witnesses included members of prominent families—Bigelow, Codman, Dana, Lovering, Sanger, Wyman. Oliver Wendell Holmes, who gave his occupation as physician, testified at some length, both for the State and the defense. For the former he said that whoever had cut up the body alleged to be that of Doctor Parkman had certainly been handy with surgical knives.

The State, of course, was attempting to prove that the remnants of human mortality which had been discovered in the vault, in a tin box filled mostly with tanbark in Webster's laboratory, and in the laboratory stove, were those of Dr. Parkman; and the defense was doing its best to prove the fragments to be those of almost anybody except Doctor Parkman.

While Dr. Nathan C. Keep was on the stand identifying the mineral teeth found in the stove to be the very same teeth he had made for Doctor Parkman, suddenly "here the City bells were rung for fire, and it being announced that the Tremont House was on fire, the Court granted an intermission, to allow the Attorney General, who boarded at the Tremont, to save his papers."

Upon resumption of the trial the spectators were given a grisly enough treat when Dr. Woodbridge Strong took the stand to discuss the matter of burning bodies. "I have dissected a good many bodies in my day," said Doctor Strong with evident relish. "I recollect a pirate I had given me one time, and as I only wanted the bones, I dissected him rapidly, and . . ." so on and on, until some of the less avid spectators left the courtroom.

Little by little, over what must have been ten terrible days for Professor Webster, the coils of circumstantial evidence could be seen closing around him, and late on the eleventh day the jury was charged by Chief Justice Lemuel Shaw, another Harvard man (1800), in an address which is still considered by lawyers to be one of the greatest expositions of the law of circumstantial evidence ever delivered, and is referred to, in the quaint way of lawyers, as *Cushing* 295. Three hours later the jury returned with a verdict of guilty. There was no demonstration, for "an awful and unbroken silence ensued, in which the Court, the jury, the clerk, and spectators seemed to be absorbed in their own reflections."

Professor Webster wasn't quite ready to greet the hangman, but his writ of error was denied, and he then addressed the Governor and Council, protesting his innocence and piously calling on the Great Searcher of human hearts as his witness. To no avail. And long before Professor Webster's neck was broken, quickly and efficiently, on August 30, 1850, he made a long confession. Janitor Littlefield had been right. Professor Webster *was* ready for Doctor Parkman, when he called on that fatal Friday. What had happened, according to Webster's confession, was this:

Doctor Parkman had come that day with the idea of getting some money. When denied it, he had called Webster both liar and scoundrel, and had shaken his fist in the professor's face. Then, said Webster, "I felt nothing but the sting of his words . . . and in my fury I seized whatever thing was handiest—it was a stick of wood—and dealt him an instantaneous blow with all the force that passion could give it." The one blow was enough. Parkman fell, bleeding at the mouth. Webster hurriedly bolted all the doors, stripped the dead man, hoisted him into the sink, and there dismembered him with the deft professional strokes that had been apparent to Dr. Oliver Wendell Holmes.

V

The Webster-Parkman affair unquestionably has had mention in more autobiographies and memoirs than any other murder case in America. The case probably comes nearer to filling the definition "classic" than any other crime in the nineteenth-century United States. Boston never quite forgave Charles Dickens for his interest in it. For, on his visit in 1869, when asked what he should most like to see of the city's great landmarks, he promptly replied, "the room where Doctor Parkman was murdered." He was taken to see it, too, by nobody but Doctor Holmes. And that evening, at a dinner tendered the distinguished Briton, Henry W. Longfellow related a singular incident regarding Professor Webster.

Longfellow had often been a guest in the Webster home in Cambridge, and on one such occasion, a year or so before the crime, Webster had the lights of the dining room lowered and a servant brought a bowl of burning chemicals which shed a ghastly luminescence on the faces of those at the table. Webster then stood up, said Longfellow, took a rope from beneath the table, and cast it around his own short thick neck, like a noose. He then leaned over the glowing bowl, rolled his eyes, lolled his head to one side, and stuck out his tongue, like one hanged. Some of the guests thought it an odd idea of entertainment.

Perhaps the best bit of folklore, though, concerns sardonic Ben Butler, to whom Harvard had failed to grant an LL.D. While cross-examining a witness in court, and treating him rather roughly, the judge reminded Butler that the witness was no less than a Harvard professor. "Yes, I know, your honor," said Ben, "we hanged one the other day."

For the next half century or more Harvard faculty members were constantly undergoing similar pleasantries, according to the late Albert Bushnell Hart, who told me that the ribbing was still prevalent in his early days at Harvard, in the 1880's. And in recent years, so Harlow Shapley reports, the chief comment on the case concerns wonder that only *one* Harvard professor has murdered another. This fact leaves the incidence of murder among Harvard faculty members very low—one in approximately every three centuries.

Actuarially speaking, the job of teaching there remains a fairly good risk.

*O*ne of the great and indestructible
phonies of the West was

The Late Calamity Jane

How many times she married, or at
least changed consorts, is beyond knowing, and perhaps beyond
belief. She appeared at different times under the style of Hunt,
Blake, Burke, White, Dorsett and Dalton, but who these gentlemen were, if they even existed, has been lost in the imperfect
records of the time and place. But the records seem to indicate
that Calamity Jane—probably—was born Martha Cannary in
Princeton, Missouri, on the first day of May, 1852. The qualifi-
cations are needed; it is best to qualify almost any statement regarding this all but indestructible character of the old West.

I like to think of Calamity Jane as the inspired person who
gave to the West its classic phrase, "Don't fence me in." I really
don't believe she uttered those words, but she lived up to them
well enough, and for forty years after the age of consent she
roamed and she ranged the West when it was wild and woolly
and when even such singularly unattractive women as she could
be sure of a bed and a bottle, and of male companionship. It will
shock all movie-goers to know it, but Jane was primarily what
is politely termed a camp follower.

Joe E. Milner, grandson of California Joe—an unpublicized
but quite genuine old scout of the plains—probably knew as
much about Jane and her career as anybody. He often related,
and even put it into print, that her father was Robert Cannary,
a farm boy who had married her mother "in a bawdy house in

Ohio to reform her, but did not do a very good job of it." The family migrated to the Montana gold fields, either in 1864 or 1865, and Mrs. Cannary died at Blackfoot a year later. What became of five other Cannary children isn't known; but Martha and her father struck out for Salt Lake City, where he too died. This left the daughter on her own, which, as her subsequent career would indicate, was exactly what she most wanted.

There are men alive today who will tell you in all seriousness that Calamity Jane was a plainsman, scout, prospector and Indian fighter without peer. They will tell you that she was a trusted scout with General George Armstrong Custer. Others will swear she served, in the form and style of a *male* scout, with Crook, with Miles, with Terry. At least one windy old character of the West told me Jane was once a scout with the Negro cavalry commanded by the then Colonel (Pecos Bill) Shafter. There is no shred of evidence to show she ever served, either as man or woman, with any military body of the United States Army— that is, not in an official capacity. The Army did not carry camp followers on its muster rolls.

Jane herself started most if not all of the stories about her noble work as a scout, and she doubtless got the idea for her romantic drolleries from an experience she enjoyed in connection with the Jenny Geological Expedition, of which, incidentally, California Joe was one of the guides. This trek was headed by Professor Walter P. Jenny, United States geologist, and went into the Black Hills in 1875 to investigate the rumors of gold there and, in the usual manner of such scientific expeditions, to make geological and topographical observations of a general nature. To protect the professors a detachment of Federal troops went along.

While the Jenny party was being formed and equipped at Fort Laramie, one of its enlisted men, Sergeant Frank Siechrist, met up with Calamity Jane who, as was her custom, liked to hang out around an Army post, or for that matter any other place where many men were congregated. Jane cottoned to the sergeant. He was not especially coy himself. Being an observant person and noting, no doubt, that Jane chewed tobacco like a trooper (she could kill a horsefly at ten feet) and in addition was shaped more like Adam than like Adam's wife, he procured a soldier's uniform for her. For all I know, Siechrist may have been a company supply sergeant. Anyhow, he got Jane rigged up in the baggy, shapeless clothes of the enlisted man of 1875, and away she went to the Black Hills with the expedition.

Sergeant Frank Siechrist had at last accomplished what more than one lonely soldier has wanted to do time out of mind. He had his wife, or at least his consort, right with him in the ranks. It was, of course, too good to last. At some stop along the way, after the party had camped one evening, an officer strolling near a stream to watch the soldiers swimming was struck dumb—we can presume—for Jane was right in there with the boys and she had troubled herself no more than they about a bathing suit. She was promptly sent back to Fort Laramie.

II

Her brief experience with the Jenny Expedition was Jane's nearest approach to being a military scout, yet on it she somehow erected the whole preposterous legend of her Indian fighting, adding to it, as the years passed, until not even a movie fan could have stomached it. She even cooked up a particularly implausible story to account for her nickname and tied it, of course, to the Army. It is a story so implausible and so pointless that I should prefer to let Jane tell it in her own words. "It was during the Indian outbreak in 1872," she related, in barrooms from Rapid City to Spokane and later in dime museums, when I was christened Calamity Jane. It was on Goose Creek, Wyoming, where the town of Sheridan is now located. Captain Egan was in command of the post. We were ordered out to quell an uprising of the Indians, and were out for several days. We had several skirmishes during which six of the soldiers were killed and several badly wounded.

On returning to the post we were ambushed. Captain Egan was hit. I was riding in advance and on hearing the firing turned in my saddle and saw the captain reeling on his horse as though about to fall. I turned my horse and galloped back with all haste to his side and got there in time to catch him as he was falling. I lifted him onto my horse in front of me and succeeded in getting him safely to the fort. Captain Egan, on recovering, laughingly said: "I name you Calamity Jane, the heroine of the plains." I have borne that name ever since.

All of which, of course, is—but never mind. Let it pass. I have no idea how she came by her name, and I am too cagey even to vouch for any of the score or more of reasons, all of them patently made up, to which long-winded raconteurs of the old West have subscribed. I'll go even further; I just don't want to hear any more reasons as to how she came by the "Calamity." If Ned Buntline had met her, I would gamble that he devised the name, just as he did that of Buffalo Bill; but I have been unable to find that Buntline ever heard of the lady.

Practically all the men who knew Jane and who left any record say that she was as able a consumer of liquor, either hard, vinous or malted, as they had ever seen, equal, in fact, to such superb topers as Bill Cody himself, a man who called for ten tumblers of redeye daily when he was himself. Men who knew her seem to be agreed, too, that she was of medium height, ruggedly built, and had brown hair and eyes. I know of but two authentic photographs of her. Both indicate a fairly husky amazon, with a very unattractive face. Unquestionably she was quite mannish, both in appearance and manner; and for all her dalliance she seems to have dressed in men's clothing during much of her life.

Like most such women, Jane was big-hearted, and on special

occasions could rise to a level above the bog of the plains under-world of which she was a part. In 1878, when there was a fearful epidemic of smallpox in the Deadwood region, she worked night and day ministering to the ill and the dying. There were few women in Deadwood at the time. Jane went from shack to shack, doling out the crude drugs she had bought herself, nursing and doctoring, preparing the dead for burial. Deadwood hailed her for it, and a quarter of a century later, when a ghostly Jane returned to die, Deadwood still remembered.

In Jane's Deadwood days her consort had been Charles Utter, better known as Colorado Charley. They lived openly together, and perhaps happily. But Wild Bill Hickok, the celebrated character who had appeared with Buffalo Bill's show and at last died in Deadwood (with his boots on), paid Jane no heed. After his death at the hand of Jack McCall, Wild Bill became a Deadwood hero and immediately went into the hagiology of the West via the dime novel route. It was then that Jane took him over, for she knew a good thing. She mourned for Wild Bill as her "departed sweetheart." She could weep copiously about it, too, and the only manner in which kindly bartenders could stem the tears was to set up a few more quick ones for Jane.

Calamity Jane was clever with horses. In 1878, after the smallpox epidemic in Deadwood, she hired out as a teamster and drove a big wagon from Rapid City to what was then Fort Pierre, now South Dakota's capital. Her employers found her competent, so long as she drove; but she had a habit of going off and getting drunk at inopportune times. For a period she lived with—that is, kept house for—a lonely rancher near Miles City, Montana, and then wandered off again. Her trail dims, then becomes clear for brief spaces. She turned up as an inmate of a bawdy house in Green River, Wyoming, and worked at the same trade for several months in Blackfoot, Montana. Then, somehow or other, she got

wholly off her range, turning up in El Paso, Texas, to marry—
so she said—a Mr. Burke, and to give birth to a daughter.

But Jane soon started working her way north to her old graz-
ing grounds. She operated briefly what she liked to call a hotel
in Boulder, Colorado, in 1893; then set out on a trek that took
her (but don't ask me what became of Mr. Burke) through Wyoming, Montana, Idaho, and into Oregon and Washington. Then,
in 1895, Jane grabbed a train of steam cars for a trip back to
the old diggings of Deadwood.

III

By the time she returned to Deadwood Jane had become a confirmed barfly and drink-cadger. One man there estimated her
daily intake at this time as two quarts of 100 proof, or anything
else on hand. All the oldtimers would buy her a few drinks every
day, though some got tired of her talk. Then, it is said, a wealthy
woman who was visiting Deadwood because of its notoriety interested herself in the aging strumpet and took her to Buffalo to
reform her. The process probably bored Jane, for she presently
disappeared from Buffalo and turned up two weeks later in
Deadwood, carrying a fearful hangover.

Jane was now something of a legend, and liars all over the
West sat up nights embellishing the story. The dime-museum
firm of Kohl & Middleton sent an agent to Deadwood to see what
sort of attraction Jane would make. He signed her up, got her
some fancy Western clothes, and on January 20, 1896, she was
presented to the public at the Palace Museum in Minneapolis.
Thereafter she toured the museums and honkytonks in many
towns throughout the West.

Show business couldn't hold her, or, more likely, didn't want
to. In 1901 Jane had fallen onto hard times indeed. In February

of that year the *Anaconda Standard,* a Butte newspaper, reported that Jane was recovering from an illness in the poorhouse at Bozeman. Apparently she had been working her way through the state by selling copies of "The Life and Adventures of Calamity Jane, by Herself," a pamphlet composed of all the fictions she could dredge from her alcoholic imagination. (I have read it—it isn't worth reading.) On this occasion Jane told the press that she had never before been obliged to accept public aid. She was still dressed in men's clothing and packed an old revolver; but her clothes were ragged and the gun long since rusty. Remarked the *Standard*: "Like the buffalo and the distinctive characteristics of the plains and mountains, she is a pathetic reminder of the vanishing glory of old pioneer days and the free and easy life of the border."

Two years later, on August 2, 1903, she died in Terry, near her favorite Deadwood. Next day the Deadwood *Pioneer-Times* reported:

Mrs. Mary E. Burke (Calamity Jane), female scout, frontier woman and one of the most picturesque characters of the early West, died in the Calloway Hospital yesterday afternoon about 5 o'clock, aged 52 years.

The *Pioneer-Times* went on gallantly to recall Jane's noble work during the epidemic of 1878, though it remained vague as to her usual occupation. The funeral was held two days later, with services in the First Methodist Church, which was packed with old settlers. A Dr. C. B. Clark delivered a funeral sermon, doing the best he could with the subject, and a Mrs. M. M. Wheeler and a Miss Elsie Cornwall sang, while a Miss Helen Fowler played the organ.

So passed the woman who probably gained more notoriety, with less good reason, than any other female character in all the old West. Her grave is not gaudy, like that of Jim Fisk up in Brattleboro, Vermont, nor is it so heavily depressing as General Grant's tomb in New York. In Deadwood, however, her grave, along with that of Wild Bill Hickok, is one of the landmarks that all visitors are sure to be shown.

*The celebrated Green Mountain Boy
was also a best seller.*

Ethan Allen, Author

AT HALF past three on the morning of
May 10, 1775, a tall man with a sword loomed out of the mist
and rushed a sentry on duty at the south port of Fort Ticonderoga on Lake Champlain. The tall man was Ethan Allen, and a
few minutes later, at the head of eighty-three Green Mountain
Boys, he mounted the stairs to the commandant's quarters, shouting profanity so dreadful that even the British regulars, who
were used to strong language, were charmed and a little stunned.
An instant later, if we are to believe Colonel Allen himself, he
delivered his deathless line about surrendering in the name of
the Great Jehovah and the Continental Congress.

What Colonel Allen actually said on this occasion is still a
matter of cherished controversy among Vermont historians.
There is, however, no doubt about the fort. Allen and his men
took it—and it was a notable feat for a mob of bushwhackers.
But the event might not have become immortal had not Colonel
Allen himself become the best-selling soldier-author of his day.
His capture of "Fort Ti" *and* his volume are what put him into
chipped marble and into the history books.

Shortly after his brilliant success at Ticonderoga, Allen and
a handful of farmers made a wholly improbable assault on the
fortress of Montreal. He was defeated, taken prisoner and loaded
with chains. For the next two years he was a captive in British
hulks, dungeons and stockades. On his exchange (at New York

in 1778) he went back to Vermont, where he was received as a conquering hero. The town of Bennington ceased all other activities, rolled out the barrel—it was rum, not beer—and gave Ethan a welcome at the Catamount Tavern that he never forgot. Nor did he recover for several days.

When his head cleared somewhat he sat down and composed "A Narrative of Colonel Ethan Allen's Captivity, Containing His Voyage and Travels, With the Most Remarkable Occurrences Respecting Him and Many Other Continental Prisoners of Different Ranks and Characters. Interspersed with Some Political Observations. Written by Himself, and Now Published for the Information of the Curious in All Nations."

Ethan Allen was unmarred by any formal schooling, and he was a gifted and natural storyteller. His "Narrative" had what it took to head the best sellers. It is a racy and swift story of what happened at Ticonderoga and subsequently. Writing almost four years after the event, Ethan quite suddenly recalled that he had demanded the fort's surrender by authority of the Great Jehovah and the Continental Congress. It was the first time this ringing piece of hyperbole appeared in print. It is also quite possible that the phrase did not occur to Ethan until he was in the throes of composition, for none of his Green Mountain Boys remembered hearing it at the time. At least two of them seemed to recall Ethan using a far different phrase—one that could not appear in print in Boston.

The "Narrative" was and still is good reading. Bombastic and modest by turns, it shows humor on almost every page. Its studied understatements and irony read as well today as when written, and the quaintness of the author's style (including a syntax often as unorthodox as it is startling) gives it a freshness that many contemporary narratives lack. Ethan relates how when he and his squad of farmers were at the gates of Montreal, two British generals at the head of five hundred trained troops, plus a band of Indians, came out to repulse them. "I perceived at once," says the author, "that this was to be a day of trouble if not rebuke." It was both. A bit later, when he is loaded down with chains and manacles, his guard tells him casually that the leg irons alone weigh forty pounds. "They were very substantial," Ethan remarks of them.

There is fighting or violence of some kind on every other page. There are monumental drinking bouts, attempted escapes, mutinies. Unspeakable cruelties are mentioned. The book has everything. Sex rears its head when two English officers plan to duel over a loose woman of Quebec City, and Ethan is to umpire the duel. He meets Lord Cornwallis and insults him to his face. "The quarterdeck is for gentlemen," says his lordship frostily. "That's why I am here," replies Ethan. To startle his guards he puts a tenpenny nail between his teeth and bites it in two. There is a zest and a naturalness throughout such as little formal writing of the time can match. It is first-class, rooting, tooting, shooting melodrama, as full of action as four reels of "Western" film, done by a master of lurid narrative. And it is thoughtfully weighted in spots with some of the best "atrocity" propaganda imaginable—stuff to make all Whigs see red.

The "Narrative" sold like buttered rum. First published as a serial in the *Pennsylvania Packet*, it was an amazing success from the first installment and was immediately (1779) put into book form by Robert Bell, "in Third Street, Phila. Price Ten Paper Dollars." (Inflation was present.) The public promptly bought every copy. Bell hurried a second printing, then a third. At the same time Draper & Folsom, in Boston, made a large printing, to be followed almost immediately by another. Three more printings were made in the following year, one each in Newbury and Danvers, Massachusetts, another in Norwich, Connecticut.

The "Narrative" sale did not die quickly, as with most war
books, but went on and on. New editions were brought out in
Philadelphia, in 1805; in Walpole, New Hampshire, in 1807;
in Albany, New York, in 1814. Subsequent printings were made,
from two to four to the decade, during the 1830's, the 1840's,
and 1850's. The last reprint I know of was made in 1930 for the
Fort Ticonderoga Museum, with an excellent introduction by
John Pell.

How much the author received for his best seller isn't known,
but it was likely little enough. He may have been paid a few
of those "paper dollars" for the serial, and possibly something
more from Printer Bell. But all of the other printings, eight of
which appeared in the author's lifetime, doubtless brought Colonel Allen nothing—except fame.

Both high and low read the "Narrative." The Rev. Jeremy
Belknap, one of New England's most illustrious writers of the
day, read the "Narrative" and found it good. He said Allen was
"an original in his way, but as Rough and Boisterous as the
Scenes he has passed through." Ebenezer Hazard said that "had
Allen's natural Talents been cultivated by a Liberal education,
he would have made no bad figure among the sons of Science;
but perhaps his want of such an education is not to be Lamented,
as, unless he had more Grace it would make him a Dangerous
member of society."

Indeed, and so it might. The "Narrative" was just something
to pass the time with. Ethan was saving his really dangerous
work until later, and in 1782, between alarums of invasions of
Vermont by the British, he sat him down in small Sunderland,
Vermont, to produce his supreme effort. His library is known to
have included Pope's *Essay on Man*, Salmon's *Geographical
Grammar*, Rathburn's *Account of the Shaker Sect*, a Bible, and
two dictionaries, one of which was Dr. Johnson's. More impor-

tant to the work in hand was an uncompleted manuscript by
Dr. Thomas Young, recently deceased, an old friend of Ethan's
and the man who coined the name "Vermont."

From these works and his own free-wheeling mind Ethan composed *Reason the Only Oracle of Man, or a Compendous System
of Natural Religion,* an odd philosophical treatise which freethinkers promptly christened "Ethan Allen's Bible." It was an
attack on theology, all theology, well in advance of Paine's *Age
of Reason.* Allen's friends the printers, Watson & Goodwin of
Hartford, Connecticut, wouldn't touch it, nor for two years would
any other printer. They knew it was dynamite. In 1785 it appeared from the press of Haswell & Russell, in Bennington, Vermont.

Only a few copies were sold, but they were sufficient to set the
parsons in full cry. They leaped to preach sermons against the
recent hero. Somebody referred to the author as "the Horned
Devil of Vermont." Paid space was taken in the newspapers to
discredit the author. And presently the Great Jehovah himself
lent a hand. Lightning struck the print shop, and nearly all of
the 1,500 copies were burned. Printer Haswell was so shaken
by the Visitation that he presently "committed the remaining
copies to the flames and joined the Methodist connexion."

Attacking the current theology called for courage greater than
that for attacking a fort. And the book, despite its small sale,
has had a sinister influence on Allen's reputation. All early biographers and historians felt it necessary to be horrified at what
they termed "certain blemishes" in his character, by which they
meant his lack of formal religion. And for the next century
many an orator, while paying tribute to Allen's courage and
ability, announced themselves distressed by his "atheistic" opinions. Even the marker on his grave, beside the Winooski River,
notes that "His Spirit Tried the Mercies of His God."

Much of the "Oracle of Reason," which appeared in a facsimile edition as recently as 1940, is amusing to read today, but more of it is hard going. Allen's "Narrative", however, remains fresh and exciting. If Hollywood ever hears of Colonel Allen his best seller will likely be good for several more printings.

A *notable drinking emporium*
was Big Fred Hewlett's

Saloon in the Timber

THE most interesting place I ever drank hard liquor in was Big Fred Hewlett's Humboldt Saloon, back in the very tall timber of Western Washington. There were bigger saloons than the Humboldt and many that boasted more brass and mirrors, but not one of them had the Humboldt's flavor. It was unique, and so was Big Fred Hewlett.

Big Fred was a State-of-Mainer. He came to Aberdeen, in the Grays Harbor country on the Washington coast, in the late nineties. He looked the situation over and decided that the hustling raw village was destined to become another Bangor or Saginaw, two of the most famous lumberjack towns on earth. He was correct. Within a few years Aberdeen, and nearby Hoquiam, were cutting a billion feet of lumber every year.

A billion feet of lumber calls for an ungodly lot of logging, and an army of loggers. Big Fred, as they say, drove his stakes, and his stakes comprised the Humboldt Saloon, which he built in that part of town lumberjacks designate as the skidroad. By the turn of the century the Humboldt was well established as headquarters for the fifteen thousand wild jacks who were cutting the cloud-crashing Douglas fir and bringing it down to Aberdeen's sawmills. It continued to be a loggers' Mecca until 1920 and Prohibition. I will come to its subsequent history a little later on.

When the Humboldt was opened, Aberdeen fairly swarmed

with cutthroats and harpies, bent on taking easy and lots of dough from the loggers on their periodic busts in town. If a cash-laden lumberjack didn't "roll" easily, his body might be found in the Floater Fleet for which the murky waters of Grays Harbor soon became notorious. During a period of approximately twenty years, there just was not any law in Aberdeen to protect the lads who blew their rolls there.

In this den of skulduggery the Humboldt was uniquely honest. Big Fred had a rule that no woman, good or bad, was ever to cross the threshold. So far as is known, none ever did. Nor were any sort of fancy men, card sharps or hangers-on allowed in the place. And when you bought a drink of whiskey in the Humboldt you had no need to fear knockout drops. The whiskey, too, was whiskey, and not alcohol colored with tea and flavored with prune juice, which was the concoction commonly served to lum-berjacks. Big Fred had his own brand, "Double Stamp" in strength as he called it, or 100 proof, and none other. On every bottle appeared a pleasing likeness of Fred, done in colors, and the same picture graced the cover of the Humboldt's boxes of cigars. Fred was a man who stood solidly behind his wares.

Big Fred's picture hardly did him justice; there wasn't room on a bottle or box for a real likeness. He stood about six feet two inches and is best described by saying he was a moose of a man and letting it go at that. His was a strong face, decorated with an elegant mustache of medium size, black as night. He wore good clothes of sober black broadcloth, a low collar with black string tie, and across his vest was strung a watch chain that was believed to weigh exactly eight ounces. He was a peaceful man, for the time and place, and never looked for trouble, but if he saw trouble coming, he met it head on.

In Aberdeen at the time was a heavyweight who had once stayed six rounds with John L. Sullivan, and he was something of a local terror. It was his custom to enter a saloon, start at the near end of the bar, and one-two, one-two—he'd knock down the drinkers, one after the other, before they knew what was going on.

Well, one day this plug-ugly reached the Humboldt. Big Fred had heard of him and was ready. As the bully came in, Fred stepped briskly around the end of the bar and came up close. "Listen, you big bum," he said quietly, sticking out his chin, "I'm the first man you knock down in here."

The big boy looked at him, apparently very surprised, but he didn't make a move. Fred went on: "Now, I'll tell you how it is in here. I don't mean to kill you but I'm planning on breaking your arm—maybe both of them. Understand?"

Fred made no move. Neither did the tough guy. The mug who had stayed six rounds with John L. Sullivan laughed nervously, then set up drinks for all hands, and departed.

"I'm glad he acted that way," said Fred. "I don't like no brawling in my museum."

Big Fred didn't like brawling and he didn't like dudes. A dude to Fred was possibly anybody who was not a logger, a saw-mill stiff or a sailor, but a dude once got into the Humboldt.

"Bartender," the dude said to Fred, "mix me a Manhattan cocktail." He couldn't have done worse. In that time and place a man who would drink a cocktail was considered on a par with a cigaret smoker, which was to say, a degenerate.

Big Fred didn't bat an eye. "What kind did you say?" he inquired politely.

"Manhattan," said the dude.

Big Fred went to work. He bit off a chew of the plug he liked and reached for a bottle. Putting one of the Humboldt's generous beer mugs on the bar, he poured a good shot of whiskey into it. To this he added a slug of gin, another of rum, a dash of real brandy, of bitters, of aqua vit', and then filled the remainder of the mug with beer. Placing this dose in front of the dude, accommodating Fred stirred it slowly with a huge forefinger.

"There, mister," he said obligingly, "is your Manhattan cocktail."

The astounded city slicker protested. "That isn't a cocktail," he began. "It's a mess of . . ."

"Drink 'er down," growled Fred, whose growl was like that of a Kodiak bear, just waking up and ornery. The dude drank to the bottom of the mug and went away.

It was one of the little things that made Fred popular.

But it was Big Fred's reputation for square shooting that got the boys coming and held them. Loggers who wouldn't think of entrusting their money to a savings bank flocked into Fred's, cashed their checks, kept what they thought they needed for the night, and turned from fifty to a thousand dollars over to Fred for safekeeping. Fred put each roll into an envelope, marked the logger's name on it, and placed it in his big safe, which had a nice oil painting of Niagara Falls on its doors.

It was common, in season, for this safe to contain as much as twenty thousand dollars, all of it the property of lumberjacks who didn't want to be rolled by the horde of pimps and bawds who infested Aberdeen. Moreover, if one of the boys returned to the Humboldt too plastered to know what he was doing, Big Fred would never allow him to draw more than five dollars. "Come back tomorrow," he'd tell the souse.

Year after year better than $600,000 in loggers' checks was cashed in the Humboldt. There is no record or rumor of a man claiming to have been shortchanged. When a man returned to the woods, he took a free bottle of liquor with him, to aid the sobering-up process. Once a week Big Fred made a visit to the Aberdeen hospital, leaving cigars—but never cigarets—to loggers who had been in woods accidents or had been beaten up in fights. It all paid dividends.

Big Fred and the Humboldt were different in other ways, too. Fred didn't go in for art. He wasn't an art lover and no fat nudes in gilt frames hung on his walls. Fred was a notable patron of the sciences, though. I spent many a happy, and fairly sober, hour in the Humboldt. Some of the boys called it the Congress of Curiosities. I liked to think of it as the Hewlettonian Institution and once told Fred so. He was immensely pleased.

In glass cases along one wall was a respectable collection of minerals from all parts of the world, labeled and classified. These specimens had come in one at a time from fellows Big Fred knew. Fred probably didn't know what "ethnology" meant but his place displayed the tribal garb, weapons and "medicine" of Indians from the Blackfeet to the Pueblo. A galaxy of ordnance included flintlocks, percussion locks, and pistols that had played parts in more or less celebrated murders and holdups. A meerschaum pipe was reputedly one that Cole Younger, the bandit, smoked to while away the long hours in the Minnesota State Prison. There was an Oregon Boot said to have been worn by Harry Tracy, Oregon's noted bad man.

Various freaks of nature were shown in bottles of alcohol. In a discreet corner was a certain part of a whale. Fred did not give this exhibit the prominence it deserved because he had become tired of hearing loggers make the same lewd or envious remarks about it. Stuffed cougars, mink, owls and snakes stared and glared at the customers. There were some pieces of huge bone, thought to have been those of a mammoth, that a lumberjack had come across in a bank of the Hoquiam River. Fred gave two quarts of his best liquor for them.

Another find was made one Sunday by two loggers returning to camp from town. Near a creek they noted a long mossy heap. It turned out to be an Indian dugout canoe. It had been there for a long time and eight inches of moss had grown over it. Near-by was the huge and ancient stump from which the dugout tree had been cut.

The two men went to Fred with the news. The stump was five hundred feet from a road. Fred gave the boys five gallons of liquor to swamp out a trail through the brush and to cut an eighteen-inch section from the stump. The markings on it looked to be those of a stone ax. Fred sent a generous slice of the stump to the Smithsonian Institution in Washington, D.C., to learn if possible what sort of a tool had been used in felling the tree, and when. The Institution could only reply that the felling had been done before 1792, when the first metal axes were brought to the Pacific Coast. Until the Humboldt's end, the stump, with the Institution's letter tacked to it, was a prized exhibit in it. Big Fred was inordinately proud of this item. "Shows what a feller could do with a stone ax when he got up a sweat," he used to say.

In time, the Humboldt museum's fame reached far places. Two men from the National Geographic Society spent several days taking pictures of Fred's collections of firearms and bows and arrows. Professors from Yale, Stanford and Cornell came to look at the old bones and other things. A number of times the Smithsonian wrote Fred about this or that. He got a big kick out of these doings for he really took a great deal of pride in his collections.

From time to time Fred spent more money in adding to the museum. From sailors he collected coins from every land on the globe. These were labeled and put into cases. Somebody toted in a hunk of meteorite from Central Oregon. Swede and Finn loggers gave him miniature ships in bottles. Fred gave a standing order to the local photographer to take a picture of every lumber schooner that docked in the harbor. He had over a hundred of them. And just before the last of the bull teams was routed from the logging woods by the coming of locomotives, Fred had the photographer go into the timber and get shots of old Cy Black-

well, the fabulous bull puncher who encouraged his oxen by leap-
ing onto the backs of the rear team and walking the full length
of ten yokes, in his calked boots, yelling like a crazed Indian.
"Some day," Fred said, "these pictures will show how the boys
used to do it."

It was probable that no town of Aberdeen's size could boast a
museum to touch the Humboldt's. Big Fred told me he calculated he had spent some $75,000 on it, and no one of the items
had cost very much. As for Fred himself, he remained a lumberjacks' saloon keeper until the end. He kept peace in his place, he
served honest liquor, and he protected patrons not only from
others but from themselves. And he set knowledge before them,
too. Many a logger got his first interest in things outside his own
narrow world from a visit to the Humboldt.

During its two decades of heyday, the Humboldt had a new
floor laid twice a year. The floor was of one and one-half inch
hemlock, a tough hardy wood. This floor, after each Christmas
and Fourth of July, was chewed into splinters by the sharp calks
in the boots of countless loggers.

It was said you could tell the state of the lumber market by
the appearance of the floor. In 1907, for instance, which was
a panic year everywhere in the country, Fred laid only one floor.

Prohibition, as I said, did away with the old place. Even before that awful day, Aberdeen had ripped up its plank sidewalks
and put down hard concrete. Loggers come to town had to take
off their calked boots—or fall and break their necks—and to
wear light shoes, same as any city slicker. Then, came Volstead.

Fred kept the place open for a few years, always at a loss, out
of plain sentiment. He sold only soft drinks, for he would not
do any sort of bootlegging. "Selling liquor is an honest business," he said, "and by God I ain't going to run no blind tiger."

Dust gathered on the finest saloon museum in the United
States. Finally, and with a sad heart, Fred closed her down. The

City of Aberdeen talked of buying the collections, but the depression came on, and little by little the museum was dissipated. I have a few of the photographs, but where the rest have gone, even Big Fred doesn't know.

Perhaps it is just as well. Today's lumberjacks like fancy joints with chromium plate, where they sit on red leather stools and do their drinking—which is often cocktails. There wouldn't be any room in such a place for Big Fred's Congress of Curiosities, not even for Cole Younger's pipe or that piece of whale that was relegated to a corner.

The funds of the First National of Northfield, Minnesota, remained intact.

The Bank the James Boys Didn't Rob

THE pleasant village of Northfield, Minnesota, as its citizens like to inform the visitor, is the proud home of Carleton and St. Olaf colleges, notable outposts, respectively, of the Congregational and Lutheran churches; and it is also, and with no qualification whatsoever, the Holstein Center of America, no less than ten thousand head of that excellent breed of horned cattle chewing their contented cuds in the community. The village, moreover, possesses the Oddfellows' State Home, ten churches, and a nine-hole golf course.

Northfield is old by Midwestern standards. It was settled in 1855 by a group composed almost wholly of New England people, and this is important to bear in mind, for the early Yankees set the character of the place which prevails, in no small part and in spite of thousands of Norwegians, to the present day. The character prevailed also and in greater degree in 1876, and because of it, on that year's 7th of September, Northfield became a town in the American legend, a place fit to compare with Lexington, Massachusetts, with Harpers Ferry, Virginia, or Johnstown, Pennsylvania, in that the towns themselves live in the shadows of the tremendous events that took place within their borders.

It was Northfield, you understand, where the celebrated James-Younger gang broke, as the saying has it, their pick. They broke it on the flinty character of the Yankees in residence there, men who did not propose to permit their First National Bank to be robbed with impunity. Nor was it robbed. In seven seething minutes that clouded the street and village square with the blue haze of exploding powder, the enraged Yankees made history. Aghast at the indecency of strangers who should attempt to steal their hard-earned cash, they shot all hell out of the raiders, killing two on the spot, wounding four, and permitting only two to escape to their native Missouri, never to attempt Minnesota again.

And lest present-day descendents of the First National's defenders grow effete and forgetful, there reposes in a fine plushlined case in a Northfield home, a relic which I have had the honor to see and which would jog almost anybody's mind. It is the authenticated right ear of one of the raiders, now desiccated and brown as an autumn leaf, but patently an ear, warning enough, surely to leave Northfield institutions alone.

II

On its great and wonderful day, Northfield drowsed in the welcome midday warmth of typical September weather. The melancholy haze of fall hung over the surrounding fields, and cicadas ground out their farewell to summer, as sad a song as is to be heard in bucolic America. Mild heat waves shimmered around the gristmill and sawmill along the banks of the Cannon river that meandered through the village.

During the noon hour, five strangers, all mounted, all wearing long linen dusters, ate dinner in a restaurant on the west side of town. They talked little but stowed away a prodigious quantity of victuals. Presently, three of them rode across the bridge into the village square, then into Division Street, where they dismounted in front of the First National Bank and threw their bridle reins over hitching posts. It wasn't quite time yet. The three strangers strolled leisurely to the corner and sat down on some drygoods boxes outside Lee & Hitchcock's store. The trio were, probably, Charlie Pitts, Bob Younger, and Jesse James.

Just before two o'clock two more strange horsemen, Cole Younger and Clel Miller, rode slowly up Division Street from the south. As they approached the First National, the trio got off the packing boxes and went into the bank. Thereupon, Miller dismounted, went up to the bank, and closed the door. Cole Younger also dismounted and pretended to be fumbling with his saddle girth.

At this moment J. S. Allen came upon the scene, a hardware merchant from his store around the corner, to deposit some money. Before he could get to the bank door, Miller grabbed him. "Stand back," he commanded.

Merchant Allen, a man of quick perception and direct action, jerked free of the stranger's grasp and ran for his store, shouting: "Get your guns, boys, they're robbing the bank!"

At that instant young H. M. Wheeler, sitting on the steps of his father's store, across the street from the bank, roused. He leaped to his feet and gave cry. "Robbers!" he shouted, "robbers!"

The preliminaries were now over, and precisely at two o'clock the show began. As young Wheeler gave his shout, Clel Miller and Cole Younger jumped to their horses and started to ride up and down the street, yelling like Comanches, shooting at everything that moved. As they rode, they were suddenly joined by three more horsemen who came out of nowhere—Frank James, Bill Stiles, Jim Younger—who also were riding and shooting and yelling.

Now the sleepy street came to life, swift and terrible, as astonished townsmen made for cover, while bullets broke windows and ricocheted from stone buildings into long mean whines that sang of death. Down went Nicholas Gustavson, a Swedish immigrant who neither spoke nor understood a word of English, a bullet near his heart.

Captain French, postmaster, looked out upon the astounding scene. He locked his doors, then started searching for a weapon. None was at hand. Being a Union veteran, he knew that something would be expected of him in this sudden emergency. He stepped into the alley behind his place, picked up an armful of sizable rocks, then went into action, heaving his missles at the two-gun wild men spreading terror in Division Street. Two other citizens quickly joined the neolithic artillery as Elias Hobbs and Justice Streator found good throwing-rocks.

Meanwhile, the raiders inside the First National were discovering the bank employees to be anything but cooperative. As the three robbers entered, Teller Bunker stepped forward—to peer into the tunnel-like openings of three of Mr. Colt's patent revolving pistols. "Are you the cashier?" demanded one of the strangers.

"No," said Teller Bunker in a tone that seemed to close the subject.

One of the guns waggled at Joseph Heywood, behind the counter.

"Are you the cashier?"

"No," said Mr. Heywood, bookkeeper who was acting-cashier. Nor would the assistant bookkeeper, Mr. Wilcox, admit to being the cashier. The three Yankee employees of the Yankee First National Bank simply answered "no" to everything and would have no further part in a conversation they obviously considered pointless. It was an impasse new to the raiders. But something had to be done at once; the uproar outside in the street was growing by the moment. The inside robbers climbed over the counter, guns ready. One of them indicated Heywood. "You're the cashier," he said, "now open up that safe, damned quick."

A second robber ran to the open vault and stepped inside. Hey-

wood jumped to his feet and attempted to slam the heavy door
of the vault. The third robber grabbed Heywood. "Will you
open that safe?" he cried.

"No. It's got a time lock." The robber belted Heywood over
the head with his gun, felling him. Then he turned on Wilcox
and Bunker who also insisted on the fiction of the time lock.

The shooting and yelling in the street rose to new heights.
Time was growing dreadfully short for the raiders.

Heywood was down on the floor of the bank. One of the robbers placed his gun close to the fallen man's head and pulled the
trigger. The bullet passed into the vault and through a tin box
containing papers and jewelry. Heywood did not stir.

Bunker and Wilcox had been compelled to get down on their
knees on the floor. During the instant the robber was firing in
an effort to frighten Heywood, Bunker took a chance. He jumped
to his feet and tore through the directors' room to the rear door
of the bank, one of the robbers close on his tail, shooting. The
second or third shot caught Bunker in his right shoulder. But he
was now in the alley.

Bunker's pursuer ran back into the bank. Wilcox was still
down on the floor. Heywood was staggering to his feet, bleeding.
Shouts and shooting outside indicated the street battle was going
badly for the raiders. The three inside bandits started to get out
of there. As they departed one of them stepped close to Heywood
and drilled him through the head—as wanton an act as ever was
committed by a member of the James-Younger gangs.

The battle in the street had indeed been going badly for the
men in the linen dusters. For one thing, young Wheeler, who had
been sitting on the steps of his father's drugstore opposite the
First National, had gone into action. He ran into the Dampier
Hotel next door, laid hands on an old Army carbine, then took
up a fine position at a second-story window of the tavern.

Storekeeper Allen, who had been prevented from entering the

bank, high-tailed around the corner to his hardware shop and proceeded to break out guns and ammunition from his stock for the rallying citizens. Nor had the embattled farmers of Lexington, Massachusetts, rallied more quickly than these Yankees transplanted in Minnesota. Dashing into Allen's place, and coming out armed with shotguns, were Elias Stacy, Ross Phillips, John Hyde, and James Gregg, loading as they ran for the scene of battle. These were angry men, furious that strangers should attempt to steal *their* money.

Northfield's other hardware merchant, A. R. Manning, had heard Allen's cry of warning. He promptly armed himself with a fine breech-loading rifle and stepped out into Division Street to find something to shoot at.

The action of the battle was swift, and brief. Streator, Hobbs, and Captain French were still heaving rocks at the five horsemen when Elias Stacy came around the corner with one of Merchant Allen's shotguns. Clel Miller was just mounting his horse. Stacy let him have it, and a handful of buckshot bloodied the bandit's face. But he mounted.

Now came Merchant Manning, bewhiskered as Moses, with his fine rifle. He up and shot the horse out from under one of the raiders, then dropped back around the corner to reload. He returned to the street of battle an instant later, now fearful with the whine and thud of bullets. Clouds of smoke whirled and eddied, hiding, then revealing the raiders. Cole Younger was nearest, and Manning shot him for a bad wound. Again, Manning dropped back to reload, then resumed his firing position, to get Raider Stiles in his sights. Taking good aim this time he shot Stiles plumb through the heart. The bandit fell from his horse dead.

Young Wheeler, peering down at the street battle from the upper floor of the hotel, now opened fire. His first shot went wild.

His second passed through what the coroner later termed "the sub-clavian artery" of Clel Miller. That worthy fell from his horse. He was dead when he hit the ground.

Out of the bank charged the three robbers to run into salvos of buckshot, bullets, and Rice County stones. Just then deadly Merchant Manning came around the corner again, rifle at the ready. Bob Younger, Colt in hand, came running toward him. At this moment young Wheeler shot Younger's gun out of his right hand. Younger picked up the weapon in his left, his right dangling uselessly, and went at Manning once more, shooting.

But it was high time to get out of Northfield. The raiders started to get away right now, Bob Younger mounting double behind his brother Cole. The battle was over. It had occupied seven minutes.

Six of the raiders were in flight, two of them badly wounded. In front of the First National lay the dead horse. A few feet away was Clel Miller's corpse, in the thick dust of Division Street. A few yards beyond lay Bill Stiles, thoroughly shot and dead. On the plank sidewalk lay poor Nicholas Gustavson, the innocent bystander, who was shortly to die. Inside the bank lay the remains of brave Joseph L. Heywood, the acting cashier who would cash nothing for strangers in linen dusters. ("Faithful Unto Death," says the bronze plaque marking the spot.)

III

The raid was over, but not the hue and cry, nor yet another battle.

The remnants of the band galloped out of Northfield by the Dundas road, leading southwest. At the farm of Philip Empey, they stole a dapple-gray horse and a saddle for Bob Younger. They rode on to Millersburg. News of the raid had not yet arrived—but it was on the way. The telegraph office at Northfield was clicking madly with the greatest story Rice County was ever to send out.

Throughout southern Minnesota farmers and townsmen left their work to swell the total number of possemen to more than a thousand. But the six outlaws were holding to the Big Woods, the long and narrow strip of mixed hardwoods that marked the region. The band pushed on into Le Sueur County. They were sighted near Mankato but escaped without a shot being fired. Then, on September 21, Oscar Sorbel, young Norwegian youth who worked on a farm near Madelia, in Watonwan County, was accosted by two strangers. He didn't like their looks. When they had departed young Oscar mounted a farm horse and rode as fast as that animal could move to Madelia village, where he sought out Sheriff Jim Glispin.

Glispin responded quickly, raising a posse and taking off immediately. The posse soon discovered the fugitives, only four in number, making their way on foot in the Hanska Slough country of neighboring Brown County, and had no trouble hemming the bandits into some five acres of ground, well covered with willow and box elder, between the Watonwan River and a steep bluff. Six volunteers, who included Sheriff Glispin, and a Captain Murphy, advanced ahead of the main posse through the thick brush. They had moved but a few yards when gunfire broke out all along their front.

This time, when the posse opened up, the action was at thirty feet. Cole Younger went down with eleven bullets in various parts of his tough body. Jim Younger fell with five wounds. Bob Younger was hit once, in the breast. Charlie Pitts was struck five times, any one of which would have been fatal. Only Bob Younger remained on his feet. "I surrender," he shouted. "They're all down but me."

Of the posse, only George Bradford and James Severson were

grazed. Captain Murphy was hit in the side but saved from a wound because the bullet was deflected by a brier pipe in his pocket—which must have nonplused the Brown County Anti-Nicotine Society.

The three wounded outlaws were locked up at Faribault for safekeeping. The body of Charlie Pitts was permitted to fall into the hands of some thoughtful medico, who removed the right ear and a portion of cheek flesh, which relics are among the cherished possessions of old Bill Schilling, Northfield's most eminent character. Old Bill also has the veritable First National safe, a bar-and-padlock job—no time lock—made by Evans & Watson of Philadelphia.

The capture of the three Youngers, the killing of Pitts, and the two dead raiders back in Northfield, accounted for all but two of the gang. Those two were almost certainly Frank and Jesse James. Frank had a badly shattered foot from the Northfield battle. He and Jesse had broken away from their fellows when the band stopped near Mankato. The two moved fast, traveling day and night on stolen horses, and turned up, on the 17th, in what is now South Dakota where they made prisoner Dr. Sidney Moshier, of Sioux City, Iowa, from whom they obtained surgical and medical aid for Frank James's wounded foot and leg.

The two James brothers then rode on, crossing the Missouri river at Springfield, and continuing as far as Columbus, Nebraska. Here they sold their horses, "took the cars for Omaha," and from there went straight to their native hangouts in Missouri.

IV

The Younger brothers served long terms in the Minnesota penitentiary at Stillwater. Bob died in prison in 1889. Jim and Cole were paroled in 1901, and the former committed suicide. In 1903 Cole was granted a pardon. He later teamed up with Frank

James in a Wild West show, and died—in bed—on March 21, 1916.

Jesse James, as almost everybody ought to know, was shot and killed by one of his own gang in 1882. Frank James lived well into the present century, dying of natural causes.

The James gang, however, was never the same after the Northfield raid. It virtually cured them of hankering after banks. They did stage one train robbery in 1879, two more in 1881; but most of the time they remained in hiding. Northfield had been their supreme disaster. And Northfield's favorite summing up of that affair is the official historian's dry remark: "The funds of the First National remained intact."

A forgotten colony of radicals
on Puget Sound were the

Anarchists at Home

ONE of the great glories of the Puget
Sound country is the serene tide-washed community of Home.
This community is fading now with a graceful nostalgic air, but
it still retains many of the spiritual vestiges of what was once
America's sole anarchist colony—in its heyday one of the most
celebrated or notorious spots in the United States. Home is never
mentioned by the booster organizations, and even the evangelical
churches have given it up as a Sodom fit only for the fires of the
Pit.

The place lies on the pretty shores of Joe's Bay, an arm of the
Sound, and is approximately 2,530 miles (as few if any crows
have flown it) west of Roxbury, Massachusetts, site of Brook
Farm, the short-lived and tremendously unsuccessful attempt
of Yankees to found a colony in the manner laid down by M.
Fourier. There is almost no intellectual connection between the
two communities, and although I know of Brook Farm only by
the vast literature that has been coming out about it for a hundred years past, I have spent considerable time at Home, right
in the bosom of anarchist families, and I should rather have
lived there than at Brook Farm. I also think it long past time
that Home Colony was called to the attention of the many Americans who never heard of it.

I doubt that the Brook Farmers had a great deal of enjoy-
ment. There was constant bickering over the division of tasks,

there was much worry over getting the substantial contributions of cash needed to support the fancy play-farmers, and the nearest thing to excitement was old Bronson Alcott's heaving in for a free meal and delivering himself of a few Orphic Sayings. It was all very daring, and quite dull. Read the Brook Farmers' own accounts, if you doubt me.

Life at Home Colony was assuredly never dull. Never. Home accepted no contributions or advice from anybody. It did not labor under the many inhibitions that plagued the Brook Farmers. In fact, Home had no inhibitions whatever, and several times it made headlines that would have shocked and stunned the pale maidens of both sexes who inhabited Brook Farm. To the good people of Tacoma and Seattle who remember it, Home was and largely is a place of smoking bombs of the Johann Most variety, and of unspeakable orgies unequalled since the times of Messalina. Yet for half a century it has successfully fended attacks by incendiary and murderous mobs, by the courts, by private detectives, Secret Service agents, and United States marshals. Jay Fox, so far as I know the sole surviving anarchist in the United States, who has lived at Home for forty years, says it has been a sort of Wild West Brook Farm, with overtones of Oneida Community and Nauvoo.

Home grew out of the failure of a socialist community called Glennis, in 1896. Fed up with the internal battles which seem to bedevil all socialist communities and also with the lazy parasites who always attach themselves to "cooperative commonwealths" three disillusioned members of Glennis, situated near Tacoma, built a boat with their own hands and struck out to cruise Puget Sound, seeking a likely spot to pitch an out-and-out anarchist paradise. These founding fathers were George Allen, University of Toronto, class of '85, O. A. Verity and F. F. Odell. They soon found a primeval spot that looked pretty good—and still does. Towering Douglas fir grew down to the beach. Ducks

swarmed in the bay. Clams held conventions there. Bees worked
on the fireweed. No man lived here, or for miles. There were
no roads. Twenty-six acres could be had from a bloated capitalist
for $2.50 an acre.

The three men mustered a total of five dollars to make a down
payment. Then Allen went to teaching school, while the others
worked at anything handy to earn money for the move. In the
spring of 1897 the Allen, Verity and Odell families, wives and
children, voyaged to Joe's Bay and began pioneering. They tore
into the gigantic trees with ax and saw, and quickly made cabins
in which to live until they could build frame houses. They also
formed the Compact, which was called the Mutual Home Colony
Association.

There was nothing of socialism in this group. The Association
was as near pure anarchism as the laws of the land would permit, and its sole reason for being was "to obtain land and to pro-
mote better social and moral conditions." It did not even attempt
to define anarchism, although Founders Allen, Verity and Odell
considered anarchism—no matter what Bakunin or Kropotkin or
Josiah Warren said—as a society so imbued with decency and
honesty that no laws were required to regulate its members.

Each member paid into the Association a sum equal to the
cost of the land he or she was to occupy, not more than two
acres to a member. The land remained the property of the Association, but the member could occupy it indefinitely simply by
paying such taxes as were imposed by the Enemy, which in this
case was the State of Washington in the style and form of Pierce
County. Any improvements, such as barns and houses, were
personal property and could be sold or mortgaged.

Like the thoroughgoing fanatics they were, the Home colonists,
as soon as they got shelter over their heads, started a paper, the
New Era, which from the start intimated that the Association had
no interest whatever in the personal lives of its members. "The

love principle of our being," said an early hand-set editorial,
"is a natural one, and to deny it expression is to deny nature."
This was clear enough, and the implied sanction of casual rela-
tionships between men and women was in time to bring an as-
sortment of cranks, malcontents and plain Don Juans. But the
early settlers were too busy with recalcitrant stumps to worry
very much about the love principle in their being, for if there
is anything to hold old Adam in bounds it is the science and art
of removing stumps of *Pseudotsuga taxifolia.* Before their homes
were finished, the busy colonists had whacked up Liberty Hall, a
sort of meeting place and school, where Founder Allen was the
first teacher.

Within six months half a dozen new families had been added
to the original three, and along came Charles Govan, a wandering printer, who proposed a new paper which should take the
colony's message to the far corners of the earth where mankind
still lived either in savagery or, worse, under imposition of State
and Capital. Govan also induced James F. Morton to leave the
staff of *Free Society,* a noted anarchist sheet of San Francisco,
and come to Home. Morton (Harvard, 1892, and Phi Beta
Kappa) was later to become a noted Single Taxer, but he was
pure anarchist when he arrived at Home, and there he and Govan
brought out the new paper under a masthead that was sheer
genius: *Discontent, Mother of Progress.*

This paper was presently to be notorious from one end of
the country to the other, but its early issues were read mostly by
other radical editors and by persons who were predisposed to
what *Discontent* said was anarchism anyway. There appears,
from a close reading of the yellowing files, to have been more
about sex in *Discontent* than about economics. A leading article
dealt with "The Rights of Woman in Sexual Relations" which,
it appeared, were many and interesting. Another piece asked
"Is 'Sin' forgivable?" It seemed that it was. The early issues

also looked at Home with a realistic eye, stating that hard work was necessary to clear the thickly timbered land, and warning intending settlers to make inquiries before coming, lest they be disappointed. There was no balm in the anarchist Gilead, simply hard work and FREEDOM (to use their typographical emphasis). *Discontent* went on to say there was nothing of socialist cooperation about Home. Everything was on a purely voluntary basis. These ex-socialists were determined they should be free of the easy-riders who had hamstrung and wrecked Glennis and nearly all other cooperative communities.

It wasn't long before *Discontent,* hand-set and hand-printed among the stumps that were still smoking, began to attract attention. Emma Goldman went to Home to lecture in Liberty Hall in June of 1899. New families arrived from San Francisco, from Virginia, from Michigan. A tract of sixty-four acres adjoining the original colony was made available at reasonable rates. A Tacoma boat line put Joe's Bay on its list of ports of call. The colonists, proud as sin, built a floating wharf and a neat shelter.

From Portland, Oregon, where they had got into trouble editing the *Firebrand,* which the courts held to be "obscene and otherwise unmailable," came Henry Addis and Abner J. Pope. A venerable man, bearded like a prophet of old, Pope called himself a Quaker-Spiritualist-Anarchist, which was quite an order but which he took easily in stride. He was soon lecturing in Liberty Hall. Addis contributed to *Discontent* a series of articles in which he came out flat-footedly for Free Love, with uppercase letters. Although the Addis articles were a bit later to get the colony into a dreadful stew, the period of 1897–1900 was on the whole active and peaceful, a very idyll of community pioneering in the backwoods. The population rose to one hundred. Deer flitted in and out of the clearings. Roosters greeted the dawn from the interminable stumps. Communist bees gathered honey for the anarchists. The hens laid famously.

Founder Allen came to have thirty pupils in his school, and he sat them down on a windfelled fir and taught them that natural laws were the only laws worth minding. He gave them Mill, Huxley, Darwin, Josiah Warren and those parts of Henry Thoreau dealing with the necessity for civil disobedience. Four who attended Allen's school have said that truancy was never known.

Presently there began a second trek of new settlers, several coming from foreign parts. Among them was Lewis Haiman, a Jewish barber from Lithuania, who married an American gentile, took two acres at Home and built a house. He also opened a shop which, he said in an announcement, he hoped would keep Homeites from looking like the cartoon conceptions of anarchists. Dances, masquerades and picnics were a part of the social life. Lectures were its meat and drink. Liberty Hall was open to all who had something to say, or only thought they did—the subject mattering not. Reconverted socialists arrived from the defunct Ruskin Colony in Tennessee, and from the Cooperative Brotherhood Colony at Burley, Washington. The Home Colony Library was organized. *Discontent*'s announcement columns began to fill up with notices of periodicals named *Freedom* (London), *Free Society* (San Francisco), and the Boston *Investigator*, founded by the celebrated Abner Kneeland, whose trial Henry S. Commager has considered in an interesting historical monograph.

II

The first shadow to fall on the industrious and intellectual pioneering colony of Home was an occurrence in far-away Buffalo, New York, where on September 6, 1901, President William McKinley fell under a bullet fired by a witless youth, Leon Czolgosz, who said he was an anarchist. A wave of hysteria swept the nation. Socialist speakers and halls were set upon by mobs. Any soapboxer on the curb was labeled "anarchist" and was

either mobbed or arrested. And then, somebody in Tacoma,
Washington, recalled that only twenty miles away was a whole
pack of wild men and women, a veritable nest of vipers, who
had never denied being anarchists.

McKinley died on September 14. On that day an anti-anar-
chist meeting was held in Tacoma, and a Loyal League formed
by members of the Grand Army of the Republic. They chartered
a steamboat, collected firearms and incendiary materials and
prepared, three hundred strong, to invade Home and put it to
the torch, with murder as a possible incidental.

Not everybody in Tacoma lost his head. Ed Lorenz, skipper
of a steamboat which called at Home, knew the colonists there
to be sober and industrious people. He went to the mob's leaders
and said so eloquently. So did the Rev. J. F. Doescher, pastor
of the German Evangelical Church in Tacoma, who had visited
Home and had found the people, in spite of their agnosticism,
which he deplored, to be honest and kindly folk. These two
heroic men stopped what might well have been a forerunner of
the melancholy tragedies perpetrated in later years in near-by
Everett and Centralia.

Thus was Home saved surely from the torch. But its troubles
were just beginning. Someone had sent copies of *Discontent* to
Federal authorities and demanded it be barred from the mails.
Post office experts in belles-lettres looked over the Home paper
and were horrified to discover that it had come out whole hog
against marriage, terming it "the lowest form of prostitution"
and adding, for good measure, that "free mating in cities of the
United States is on the increase and the ecclesiastics cannot seem
to halt it." There was even a trace of gloating in the article,
which was one of those contributed by Henry Addis, who was not
even a member of the Home Colony.

So, packing a gun on each hip and wondering what size of
bombs he should have to dodge, a United States marshal went

over to Home to arrest *Discontent*'s editors and contributors. Hearing that the Law was on the way, the colonists met him at the Home wharf with a delegation of welcome, including pretty little flower girls, took him to one of the homes for an excellent anarchist supper, then made him the guest of honor at a whopping big dance in Liberty Hall. The astonished officer put away his guns and thoroughly enjoyed himself, remaining overnight. In the morning he returned to Tacoma with his prisoners, and reported that he had never met more agreeable people than in Home, or had a better time.

The *Discontent* staff stood trial and were freed by an understanding judge, who ordered the jury to sign a directed verdict of acquittal. It was a clear victory for Home Colony, but a year later it lost its post office, by order from Washington, and Home folks have since, and to this day, had to get their mail at Lakebay, two miles distant. Another blow quickly followed the loss of the post office: *Discontent*, which Federal authorities held to have been the mother of altogether too much progress, was forbidden the mails.

The rumpus had another and more cheerful result. It called national attention to Home, putting it briefly if luridly on the front pages of big-city newspapers, and Home went into a boom. Henry Dadisman, well-to-do farmer, arrived and bought two hundred acres next to the Association land, which he threw open to settlers at cost. A Minnesota widow came, built a fine farmhouse, and settled down. Families came from Indiana, and during the 1902–1907 period, more Russian Jews arrived to take up colony or Dadisman land. A new Liberty Hall, much larger than the first, was built; and a co-op store, still flourishing, was opened.

When *Discontent* was barred from the mails, Editor Morton merely changed the masthead to read the *Demonstrator*, and kept the editorial policy intact. In the light of Home's new notoriety there started a flow and ebb of eccentrics that has made the place one of the most interesting spots on all Puget Sound. This period at Home, indeed, deserves the serious attention of some scholar who is interested in the manner in which old and new radical theories permeated the utmost reaches of the United States at the beginning of this century. Here was a tiny community, set in the deep woods in the northwestern corner of the Republic, as remote from the intellectual centers as possible, and reached by an awkward boat trip, or by mere mud trails. Yet Home's Liberty Hall shook and shimmered with virtually every intellectual breeze one could name, while the colonists listened to and often argued with a continuous congress of cranks and prophets.

III

From Chicago to Home came somewhat moth-eaten agents for Koreshanity, the otherwise forgotten philosophy-religion founded in 1886 by Dr. Cyrus R. Teed, to reveal the True Faith to Homeites and incidentally, as part of their belief, to prove that the earth is a hollow ball and that we live on its inside, the quickest way to China being straight up into what we call the atmosphere.

Then came Professor Thompson, no first name, perhaps the mogul of all individualists, who walked down the Home gangplank one afternoon displaying a magnificent beard but the dress and other garments of a woman. Professor Thompson was male enough; brawny and tough, he immediately went to work chopping wood. That night he gave a rousing lecture on the need, if the world were to make any progress, for all to wear women's clothing. It was more aesthetic and comfortable, he maintained.

From California came the then celebrated Lois Waisbrooker, author of a strange book entitled *My Century Plant*, a work that revealed how to free the world from "the disease of Sex." She

liked Home, took an acre, and settled down in company with
Mattie D. Penhallow, a noted radical of the day, to get out a
very odd sheet called *Clothed with the Sun*. I regret much that
I have failed to find a copy of this periodical. Old-timers of
Home inform me it was a humdinger, even for anarchists, and
reported all of the facts of life in no mealy-mouthed manner.
It didn't last long. The post office department took one look at
it, and presently a whole delegation of United States marshals
swarmed into the colony like locusts and carted off the two
maidens, one of whom was indicted, convicted and fined. It was
one more case of "unmailable matter."

The place was now rolling high. Home and its odd residents
and visitors were good for a story in almost any newspaper and
periodical in the country. College professors came to see and
write learned pieces. The *Independent*, a national magazine of
wide circulation, sent a man to Home, who reported favorably
on the place and remarked it was the most sensibly managed of
any community attempt he knew. It had 170 adult members.
Work was exchanged at the rate of fifteen cents an hour, although
no cash changed hands. The co-op store was doing well. So were
the Home logging operators.

After her conviction in the *Clothed with the Sun* affair, Miss
Waisbrooker returned to Home and promptly started getting out
another sheet, this time called *Foundation Principles*. I haven't
been able to get the faintest idea what it was about, but Jay Fox,
who can be ribald at times, told me he thought it was "the same
old subject, Adam and Eve."

Elbert Hubbard, no slouch himself as a community man,
made the trip to Home from East Aurora, New York, to stay
several days and to lecture nightly in Liberty Hall. Colonists
found him heart and soul in sympathy with the colony, and later
he spoke good words for it in a characteristically graceful and
inaccurate piece in the *Philistine*. Emma Goldman, famous now

since McKinley's death, came to Home a second time. Moses Harmon, the old-time crusader for almost any unpopular cause, and editor of *Lucifer*, which advocated the use of contraceptives, came to recuperate at Home from his several incarcerations in the prisons of Illinois and Kansas.

Meanwhile, children had been born in Home of legally married couples, and their very given names reflect the faith of their radical parents. Listen to the roll: Albert Parsons Grosse, William Morris Grosse, William Morris Snellenberg, Emma Goldman Falkoff, and Eugene Debs August. There was also Radium LaVene, who has told me that the Homeites, like many others, were much taken with the news of the discovery of radium and felt it would be a good name. Radium LaVene's brother was first named Revolt LaVene, but a bit later became Francisco Ferrer LaVene, honoring the Italian school-reform martyr. These boys and girls, now grown, recall a welcome visitor to Home in Dr. Ben Reitman, who used to gather them around a fire on the beach to tell them ghost stories, then to show how the seemingly supernatural always had a rational solution. Harry Kemp came too, to get material for his *Tramping on Life* and his poems. Big Bill Haywood, fresh from his acquittal in the Steuenberg murder case, came to Home to spend several weeks, and of course to speak in Liberty Hall.

What a yeasting it was, the boiling and bubbling at Home! Spiritualists came, and one remained to set up in business. A school in Esperanto was opened. Exponents of various food fads came and went, among them one Dr. Hazzard, an eloquent female who spoke to such effect that John Buchi, Swiss butcher at Home, wished "a Got damn on all der wegitarians." Local enthusiasts started a Class in Hatha-Yoga, another in straight theosophy. Russellites came to report the imminent end of things, which was all right with the anarchists. Pantheists, Freethinkers of all shades, Monists, Mormon missionaries—they all came, and

Home gave them all a hearing. One Homeite, Laura Wood, set up housekeeping in an Indian wigwam; another, Joe Kapella, went to live in a tree for several months. It all must have been quite wonderful. Brook Farm had nothing like it.

IV

The great activity at Home Colony did not go unnoticed around the Sound, and stories of horrible sex orgies became current and popular with orthodox Washingtonians. Much of the talk stemmed from articles in the uninhibited *Demonstrator*, as untrammeled as a yearling Durham bull put to pasture in May. It seldom appeared without a few remarks on something very similar to free love. The colony itself never held any canons regarding the desirability or undesirability of free love. That there were domestic arrangements in certain homes of Home which had not received the benefit of either church or state was of common knowledge, but they were neither sanctioned nor condemned.

Meanwhile the Philistines were gathering their forces. Their next attack occurred in 1910, and is still referred to as the Great Nude Bathing Case. The colony had by then split into two factions over the subject of landholding. This was settled, amicably on the whole, and each member was given a deed to his two acres. The Association was dissolved, although Liberty Hall and the co-op store were continued as community enterprises. The store, indeed, may have been a factor in attracting to the colony a number of farmers who liked the low prices at the Home co-op but had no sympathy for Home's live-and-let-live policy. In any case, it was from these latecomers that a complaint came to the county authorities, naming names and charging that certain Home anarchists were bathing in the nude, men and women together.

The charges were true enough. The simple Russians who had come to Home many years before brought their samovars with them, and also their custom of nude bathing. It had been going on at Home for a decade, without scandal. But now, because of the Philistines, one man and four women were arrested and found guilty on charges of indecent exposure. The trials made front page news in almost all sections of the country. Home was again in the papers.

At this time Home had a new paper, the *Agitator*, edited by the aforementioned Jay Fox, a radical who dated back to the Haymarket Bomb in Chicago. Fox had long been an agitator and organizer of left wing labor groups. He still carried in one shoulder a bullet that had been fired in the McCormick Harvester strike in Chicago in 1886, and he had been active in the I.W.W. and in the rambunctious shingle-weavers' union in the Northwest woods. He was also an able journalist, and now he came out with a sizzling editorial, "The Nudes and the Prudes," in which he more than suggested that all lovers of liberty should ostracize the persons who had brought the charges of indecent exposure. Editor Fox was hauled off to jail and charged with "encouraging or advocating disrespect for law." The prosecution naturally brought "anarchy" into the case and played up Home's reputation in a successful effort to convict Fox, who was sentenced to two months in Pierce County Jail. On appeal, the state supreme court upheld the verdict.

Now the wobblies, the I.W.W., and other radical groups the country over took up the case and made it into a national *cause célèbre* in all liberal circles. The Free Speech League, forerunner of the Civil Liberties Union and headed by such well known persons as Leonard Abbott, Brand Whitlock and Lincoln Steffens, joined the battle. Dances and rallies for the "Jay Fox Free Speech Fight" were held from Boston to Portland, Oregon, and money raised for an appeal to the United States Supreme Court,

which found the verdict proper. Fox gave himself up and went
to jail for six weeks. Then he was given an unconditional pardon
by Governor Lister of Washington. He returned to Home and resumed publishing the *Agitator*.

Next came the McNamara case. One night in October of 1910,
the building of the Los Angeles *Times* was wrecked by an explosion that took twenty-one lives and was followed by the sen-
sational confessions of the two McNamara brothers. Also im-
plicated was one David Caplan, and a vast man hunt was set in
motion to find him. Presently at Home there appeared a tall,
suave and handsome book agent who was peddling one of those
sets of home encyclopedias (170,000 pages, beautifully illustrated, fine bindings) without which no home, not even an anarchist's home, could be said to be complete. The tall agent circulated around Home for several days. Mrs. Lewis Haiman recalls
that when she went to the door, and kept the man safely on the
outside, he appeared to be far more interested in peering over
her shoulder to see who was inside, than in selling his array of
the world's knowledge. He was, of course, the famous William
J. Burns, the detective, looking for the missing Caplan. Fugitive
Caplan was taken later, though not at Home, and given ten years.
In Burns's memoirs, published not long before his death in 1932,
the detective devotes several pages to his days as a book agent
in Home.

During World War I, Home was infested by marshals and
secret agents of the United States government, some with false
whiskers, some plain, but all of Home's citizens managed to
keep out of their clutches. In the more recent war, so quiet had
Home been for two decades, it was never under suspicion.

Today Home is, as it must always have been, a charming
place in which to live. The last of the Founding Fathers, George
Allen, died in 1944, well into his eighties. Dead, too, is Tom
Geeves, the patriarch of Home, as whiskered as any legendary

Nihilist, who had wandered ashore from a British ship, circa
1910, and for no doctrinaire reasons, but simply because he
liked the place, had taken abode in an old shack at Home. There
he lived to be almost one hundred and nine years of age.

The younger generation of Home, for the most part university graduates, have gone away and married. Many are in California where each year a Home picnic, staged by Radium La-
Vene, now a Los Angeles businessman, draws up to a hundred
old Homeites and their children.

Jay Fox, perhaps the last of the veritable anarchists, genial
and mellow at seventy-seven, lives on in Home and is writing his
memoirs, while his wife, Cora, spends her talented spare time
hand-painting and glazing chinaware of such beauty that it is
sought after by the wives and daughters of Seattle and Tacoma
capitalists.

The outlander visiting Home is sure to find it pleasant, both
physically and socially. The Home Colony tradition is still
strong. These are well-read people. When you come across two-
acre farmers conversant with Mill and Bentham and Marx and
Dewey and Emerson and Thoreau, as well as with poultry feed
and beehives, you know you are in no orthodox rural community. There are Homeites today who teach art and music.
There is much professional interest in and practice of crafts, especially of weaving. Bees, hens and ferns are the chief sources
of agricultural income.

Over all is a feeling, not of revolution, but rather of a lack
of interest in political movements. It would not be fair, however,
to include Jay Fox in this placidity. The fires of Revolution still
burn in the old anarchist, perhaps the last of his kind, and he is
happy when William Z. Foster, more in direct touch with the
world, comes to visit him, as he does occasionally, and tells him
how goes the battle with the minions of Capital.

The man who invented the dime novel and Buffalo Bill.

Life and Times of Ned Buntline

NED BUNTLINE invented the dime novel and wrote 410 of them to prove that a new art form had arrived. He also invented the character of "Buffalo Bill" and draped it on William F. Cody, who ever after lived in a thick fog of wonder, honestly incapable of discriminating between what actually had happened in his life and what Buntline swore had happened. Buntline's own life was more exciting than any of the fiction he wrote, and also gamier by far. He lived, as the phrase had it, a full life, and died at sixty-three, probably from the effects of extended lead poison from the many bullets still in his body when at last he turned his face toward the wall.

Ned Buntline was really Edward Zane Carroll Judson, born in 1823 in Stamford, New York, on a night, says one of his biographers, that was wild and fearful to behold, when the floodgates of heaven opened wide and added to the fury of a tremendous electric storm of such power as to make spectators tremble. This kind of night was much favored by biographers of the day to usher in the birth of an adventurous soul such as Judson was to become, and none more deserved a turbulent and tempestuous introduction than he.

Judson's father, Levi, was a stern and unyielding man of old Yankee stock who tried to run his nineteenth-century home according to the rules and customs set up in Massachusetts Bay Colony two hundred years before. Young Judson did not like the restrictions. He loved to fish and hunt. His folks did manage to keep him in school for portions of a few years, but when his father told the son he was to study for the law, the boy ran off to Philadelphia and there shipped as a cabin boy for a trip around the Horn.

Young Judson liked the sea. On his return he enlisted as an apprentice in the United States Navy. For courage and resourcefulness in rescuing several members of the crew who had been run down in a longboat by a Fulton Ferry steamer in the East River, he was commissioned midshipman by President Martin Van Buren. In 1842, after a number of escapades which had brought disciplinary measures, he resigned from the Navy. In the meantime, under the signature of Ned Buntline, he had written an account of an incident on shipboard which appeared as a small book, *The Captain's Pig*. The book made something of a noise and attracted the attention of Lewis Gaylord Clark, editor of the *Knickerbocker Magazine*. For this periodical he did several more stories.

During 1843–1844 Judson was probably where he claimed to have been—a sort of freebooting soldier and marine in the Seminole War. Next he appeared in the Far West as an employee of the Northwest Company, and claimed to have done a prodigious amount of hunting, killing many bison, mountain goats and a few grizzlies. He couldn't have been a commercial hunter very long, for in 1844 he started a periodical, *Ned Buntline's Own*, in Cincinnati. Apparently only one issue appeared. For the next six months he edited six numbers of Lucius Hines's bid for culture, *Western Literary Journal*, and then decamped, leaving Hines to pay the numerous bills.

Presently Judson turned up in Eddyville, Kentucky, where he married a woman described for posterity only as "Seberina," who died within a few weeks; and at Gallatin he performed the notable feat of going into the woods to pursue three men wanted in connection with a particularly atrocious murder. He overtook two of them, tied them to trees, then went on to chase the third who, however, got away. Judson took the two wanted men to Gallatin and received $600 reward.

With the reward cash in his pocket, Judson went to Nashville, Tennessee, and again tried the publishing business with a second version of *Ned Buntline's Own*, a sheet devoted largely to matter of a scandalous nature. It was not long, however, before the venture was interrupted by what he termed "distractions incident to moving the periodical to New York City." This was a gross understatement: the "distractions" actually referred to one Robert Porterfield, a quick-triggered scion of Southern nobility who accused Judson of tampering with the affections of Mrs. Porterfield. Mr. P. made the grievous error of waving a revolver while talking to Mr. Judson.

Now, if a man were quick enough, he might shoot Judson; but it did not do any good simply to display a gun, for Judson did not frighten easily, or at all. On this occasion he very promptly shot and killed Mr. Porterfield, then surrendered to the authorities, saying the killing was the result of a formal duel. While he was being arraigned in a Nashville courtroom, Porterfield's brother entered, shooting as he came, and putting three bullets into Judson. Not having a gun handy, Judson tore out of the courtroom and took refuge in a near-by hotel; and right behind him came Porterfield leading a mob. Bleeding from his wounds, and still unarmed, Judson was chased down the hotel corridor by the mob, then leaped out a third-story window and crashed onto the street.

Now the mob had him. They threw a rope over the beam of a sidewalk awning, and strung Ned Buntline Judson as high as Haman, though not quite so well. His neck failed to snap, and before he could quite strangle to death the sheriff cut him down and was permitted by the mob to cart away what they believed to be the dead body of a loathsome Yankee.

Although Judson admitted his neck was a trifle sore, he appeared again in the courtroom, this time to face the grand jury, which refused to indict him. Thus were his Nashville "distractions" ended, and Judson gladly moved on to New York, where he rented a room on Spruce Street and resumed publication of *Ned Buntline's Own*. He also started turning out paperback books that sold for ten cents and presently became known as dime novels. *The Black Avenger, The Virgin of the Sun* and *The Volunteer*, all appeared in 1847. Judson was a fast worker.

In the meantime, Judson's periodical took on a new flavor. Instead of scandalmongering, Editor Judson came out strong for the Common Man, specifically the common, white, native American man who, so Judson said, must organize his kind or go down before the hordes of German and Irish immigrants then flooding the country. Taking on Marcus Cicero Stanley, one of the ornaments of the *National Police Gazette*, as an associate editor, Judson fanned the fears of native Americans with some of the hottest jingo literature of the period. With editorial, cartoon and fictional "news stories" masquerading as fact, he prepared the natives of the Eastern states for the coming of the Native American or Know-Nothing political party, soon to sweep the nation.

During a few months in the Mexican War period, Judson was away from New York and may well have been where he said he was—serving as a spy and scout in Mexico. One can never be sure about Judson. In any case, he was soon back in New York, beating his drum, this time with at least one specific menace with which to inflame his readers. The menace was a distinguished English actor named William C. Macready.

II

The Bowery idol of the 1840's was a native American actor, Edwin Forrest, a Herculean figure of a man with the voice of a bull and no little vanity, who had been certified at numerous banquets over the years as America's first man of the theater. Incidentally, Forrest was also the First American actor to have invaded the British Isles, where he had been treated most hospitably by Macready, England's first tragedian, but had also been hissed on several occasions. And now, in 1849, Macready was making a tour of the United States, playing Shakespeare and other alleged highbrow plays. It might be pertinent to mention that Macready was probably as vain as Forrest and as quick of temper.

Editor Judson, as already noted, was using *Ned Buntline's Own* to muster native Americans against the damned foreigners. He had also, oddly enough, become something of a hero to the members of Mike Walsh's Empire Club, a Tammany Hall affiliate, by knocking cold a couple of Walsh's gorillas in a Bowery barrel house. Although a goodly portion of the lower levels of Tammany were "foreigners" who had been born in Ireland, Judson saw nothing inconsistent in using them for a demonstration against English foreigners. His periodical was presently pointing with horror to the fact that so-called Americans were paying money to see an English actor. This, he indicated, was subversive to the Republic.

Judson and Edwin Forrest had been warm friends for several years. Whether or not Forrest egged Judson into his attacks on Macready is not known. Judson was perfectly capable of finding his own targets anyway; and he proceeded to snipe at Macready as the Englishman toured New England and the Midwest and, at last, in April of 1849, came to New York City. Here he was to fill an engagement at the new and rather swell Astor Place theater, built the year before at the point of the triangle formed by Lafayette Place, Eighth Street and Astor Place. That same April Forrest was appearing at the Broadway theater, near Pearl Street.

The Astor Place house had proved to be a white elephant. Its eighteen hundred seats were seldom filled, partly because of a rumor that one could not occupy a seat there unless one appeared in evening clothes. This was quite untrue, but the rumor is important because it helps to set the scene for what was about to happen by indicating the snooty reputation of the Astor Place house.

Editor Judson continued to remark in his periodicals, and often in CAPITAL LETTERS, which semiliterates always find inflaming, that British actors were taking the bread out of honest American actors' mouths. On the morning of April 23, the day Macready was to open at the Astor Place, a leading plug-ugly of the Empire Club was on hand, when the box office opened, to purchase fifty tickets; and all day long men who did not look like Astor Place habitués continued to buy tickets in twos, in fours, and in dozens. When the curtain went up that night on *Macbeth* a drama critic present remarked that at least one third of the audience patently did not belong there.

Macready made his first appearance in the third scene. Eggs, old shoes, then chairs rained upon the stage, accompanied by cheers for Edwin Forrest and groans for Macready. After trying vainly to get on with the show, Macready rang down the curtain. The morning papers took Macready's side, and one of them said that Forrest was the instigator of the disturbance. As for Macready, he said he had had enough of New York; but when Washington Irving and a group of the city's most eminent men had signed a public petition, asking him to go on with his engagement, the actor agreed to resume.

On the day Macready was to reopen at the Astor Place house placards suddenly appeared on walls throughout Manhattan. They asked if Americans or Englishmen were to rule New York, and went on to announce that the crew of a British Cunarder then in port had threatened all Americans "who shall dare to express their opinions this night at the English Aristocratic Opera House," by which the Astor Place theater was meant. Then the placards sounded the tocsin: "Workingmen, Freemen, Stand by Your Rights!"

It is possible, even probable, that Judson wrote and published the placards. Incidentally, there was absolutely no truth in the allegation about the British sailors.

The Astor Place management, however, prepared for trouble. They battened down the hatches as well as possible, boarding up the theater windows and asking the city for a detail of two hundred policemen. Somebody in authority also called for troops, and a regiment of militia took up positions in the street.

The performance opened with every seat filled. Mr. Bennett's man from the *Herald* noted that only seven of the eighteen hundred seats were occupied by women. This was to be an evening for males. Heckling began as soon as the curtain went up. The cops pulled the hecklers from their seats and took them to the theater basement, where a sort of guard room had been improvised. On went the show, with only minor disturbances until, suddenly, the planks over one of the windows gave way and cobblestones rained into the house from the street. Outside a vast mob was on the loose. Beaten with clubs and stones, the militia at last opened fire in deadly earnest. The mob broke and dispersed, leaving twenty-three dead or dying in the street, and twice as many wounded. Among the hundred or so persons arrested was Editor Judson, who denounced what he termed interference with a gentleman of the working press.

Actor Macready was smuggled out the stage door in disguise, then mounted a horse and rode as fast as he could to New Rochelle. From there, next day, he went to Boston, and so home to England.

For a man who ordinarily was both vocal and eloquent, Judson acted in an odd manner at his trial, at which he was charged

with inciting and leading the attack on the theater. He refused
to take the witness stand. He was found guilty and fined $250,
and received sentence of a year in the jail on Blackwell's Island.
Throughout his incarceration Judson remained a hero to the
Bowery boys, and his release was an event of the first magni-
tude. He was met at the door of the jail by an immense crowd,
many of whose members had managed to struggle into clean
shirts with neckties. Two brass bands played exultantly. This
escort saw Judson safely back to Manhattan where a monster
testimonial banquet was staged, with oratory until all hours.

III

Judson now became a leading organizer of the Native American or Know-Nothing party, which offered candidates for every
office in the land from county sheriff to President of the United
States. He went to St. Louis in 1852 to "help" with a city election there, and was presently indicted for causing a riot during
which a number of citizens were killed, two houses burned and
much other property destroyed. He got out of this jam by skip-
ping bail.

When the Know-Nothing party collapsed in 1856, Judson
bought some wild land in the Adirondacks and there built a big
house which he called the Eagle's Nest and which he used as
headquarters for many hunting and fishing expeditions. Meanwhile, he had continued to turn out dime novels by the bale—
*The Mysteries and Miseries of New York, Cruisings Afloat and
Ashore, The Red Avenger, Life on the Plains* and many others.

During this period he once wrote a book of 610 pages in sixty-
two hours, neither eating nor sleeping until it was done. He told
a friend he always thought up a good title for a story, then wrote
the story, swiftly. "I take a bound book of blank paper," he
said, "then set my title at the head of it. I push ahead as fast

as I can, never blotting out anything and never making a correction or a modification. . . . If a book does not suit me when I have finished with it, I simply throw it into the fire, and begin all over again without reference to the discarded text." Judson earned a lot of money by this method.

He got into the Civil War rather late, enlisting in September of 1862 in the first New York Mounted Rifles. His war record is quite obscure, but it is certain he was discharged in August of 1864 on a War Department special order. His record was "thoroughly discreditable." Upon discharge he set out at once for New York where he announced to his many admirers he had served in the war "as chief of scouts with the rank of colonel." Thereafter he was known as Colonel Judson.

In 1869 Colonel Judson performed the greatest service of his long and busy career. On a buffalo hunt out of Fort McPherson, Nebraska, he met a tall, lithe, unknown and very handsome plainsman named William Frederick Cody. Judson was charmed, and presently Cody became Buffalo Bill, the remarkable hero of a remarkable series of stories by Ned Buntline. A bit later Judson persuaded Cody to meet him in Chicago. Here, in the space of four hours, Judson wrote a whole play, *The Scouts of the Prairies,* rehearsed it twice, engaged a theater, and produced a show featuring Buffalo Bill that ran, in Chicago and New York combined, for more than two years.

When the run was over, Buffalo Bill was a national character, a glorious symbol of Frontier America, and so he remained until his death almost half a century later, a creature out of the uninhibited imagination of Colonel Judson, alias Ned Buntline.

Judson lived on until 1886, still writing tripe at the Eagle's Nest, still fishing and hunting and entertaining lavishly. His character must have been more than commonly filled with conflicts, for his friends and enemies were both many and staunch. He appears to have been a good friend himself, and an implacable enemy. He was, said Fred M. Pond (Will Wildwood), who knew him well, a big-hearted, genial and always entertaining soul.

Judson died with his boots off, as nearly as I can surmise from various accounts, from a large number of bullets which had at various times been shot into him by outlaws, mobsters, assorted gangsters, Confederate soldiers, Indians, and relatives or husbands of seduced maidens and wives. There were also a few complications, including sciatica, angina pectoris and liver complaint. Taken all together, they were enough to lay him by the heels who was apparently immune to hemp and hot lead. At least two of his four wives survived him, and so did the most magnificent character he had ever created, Buffalo Bill.

A forty-two-piece band was none too loud for

A Salute to Buffalo Bill

THE United States Senate enjoyed a refreshing half-hour when the Gentleman from Wyoming, Mr. Edward V. Robertson, was given the floor and stood up to pay centennial tribute to the memory of the late William Frederick Cody, the one and only Buffalo Bill, who was born in Scott County, Iowa, in 1846. It is possible that a few of the younger senators needed to be told that Buffalo Bill was one of those rare characters who become legends while they still live, people like John L. Sullivan, Jesse James and lovely Lillian Russell, though Buffalo Bill was greater than any of these.

It was proper and very decent of Senator Robertson to remind his harassed colleagues of a happier time, a day when a long-haired man in buckskin with a Colt .45 and not a professor with two ounces of uranium was the most important American; and I fancy that the solons enjoyed the reminder and were indeed refreshed, although nostalgic sadness must certainly have fastened upon the elder of them. But I wish that the senator from Wyoming could have dropped at least a footnote to the memories of the two men who took Bill Cody and made him into Buffalo Bill —a couple of homemade press agents named Burke and Judson. We shall not see their like again. Without them, Cody would be merely an entry in the yellowing files of the United States Fifth Cavalry records.

Let it be understood that this writer has no desire to dim the luster of Buffalo Bill. I would as soon heave a brick at the memory of dainty Annie Oakley, whom I once saw in Mr. Keith's theater in Boston, after which I went away charmed for life. I also saw Buffalo Bill when the "Original Wild West" set up its tent at White River Junction, Vermont, and though I had already gazed upon the magnificence of Admiral George Dewey and gaped at Niagara Falls, the memory of the one blew away in the mist of the other, wholly blotted out by the dazzling sight of Buffalo Bill.

The memory of Bill and Annie is secure so long as a man lives who saw them; but Burke and Judson are recalled only by persons of antiquarian leanings or by those who have read of their great labors for Buffalo Bill in the amusing books by Frederic E. Pond (*Life and Adventures of Ned Buntline*) and Richard L. Walsh (*The Making of Buffalo Bill*), both of which cry aloud for reprinting.

II

Although Bill Cody's tombstone says he was born in 1845, the Cody family Bible places the event on February 26, 1846. While Bill was still a youth his family moved from Iowa to Kansas, and the boy, who refused to attend school, went to work as a sort of messenger for the celebrated overland freighting firm of Russell, Majors & Waddell. While so engaged he was said—much later—to have taken part in an affray with Indians and to have killed one of them. Bill was then almost eleven years old. The story is doubtful. On it, however, press agents Burke and Judson erected the whole structure of Buffalo Bill the Indian Killer, as bloody a saga as ever appeared in print. In time even Cody came to believe it. Incidentally, it is only fair to remark here that Cody was no liar: he was merely susceptible to suggestion, and Burke and Judson were two of the most proficient suggesters imaginable.

If Cody learned to kill redskins at an early age, he also learned to down liquor. Not his press agents, but his sister Helen told of a boyhood binge after which he arrived at home late in the night, singing, shouting that he was going to be President of the United States. She added: "Will never touched hard cider again." Possibly he didn't, but one should not take the statement to mean that Bill did not touch liquor, for he became and remained to the end one of our really great topers. In his prime (which endured for many years), he required ten tumblers of good stout whiskey a day, as he often remarked, to keep his kidneys functioning properly. Probably he was right, too, so far as the medicinal properties of liquor were concerned, for Gene Fowler, who knew Bill in his later days and saw him down incredible draughts of straight whiskey even then, said that no amount of hard liquor could bloat his stalwart figure, crimson his notable nose or otherwise rob him of the charms that made the hearts of women flutter alarmingly.

From his messenger-boy job young Cody went to riding for the Pony Express. He served briefly with a company of jayhawkers who were harassing the secessionists of the region, but he did not enlist in the Union Army until early in 1864. He often related to friends how it had happened. "One day," he said, "after having been under the influence of *bad* whiskey, I awoke to find myself a soldier in the Seventh Kansas Volunteers."

Cody's war service, during which he rose from the rank of recruit to that of full private, was neither bloody nor spectacular. It was in 1867 that he took on the job that was to give him his nickname. Goddard Brothers, food suppliers to the construction crews of the Kansas Pacific Railroad, hired him to kill bison. In this occupation he was supreme. In seventeen months, by his own account, which may well have been an understatement, he shot 4,280 bison. He had certainly earned the title that was to be his, yet he still did not have it. His first press agent was still two years in the future.

After the bison-killing period, Cody became a civilian scout with the Fifth Cavalry. Unquestionably he was an excellent scout, both shrewd and brave, and a dead shot to boot. In a number of skirmishes with Indians he performed well enough to be cited by General E. A. Carr and also by General Phil Sheridan. Yet the man who really came out of these battles a hero was not Bill Cody but Major Frank North, perhaps the greatest Indian fighter of them all. Major North's name was constantly mentioned in dispatches. The newspapers took him up. And presently there arrived at Fort McPherson, Nebraska, where Major North was stationed, a character known to thousands of semiliterates by the nom de plume Ned Buntline, the inventor of the dime-novel school in American literature.

Buntline, who was in fact the aforementioned Judson, found Major North diffident. No, he did not wish to appear in any of Buntline's stories. Nor could Buntline persuade him. "The man to fill that bill," North said coldly, "is under that wagon." The man under the wagon was Bill Cody.

III

When Ned Buntline met Cody in 1869, the Buntline stories were in great vogue. He saw in the handsome young scout just what he needed as the central figure in a new series that would deal with life on the American frontier. Kit Carson, Davy Crockett, Daniel Boone—all were dead. It was time for a new hero.

Before he left Fort McPherson Buntline had given Cody the name of Buffalo Bill, and presently Buntline's new serial was tingling his many readers with *Buffalo Bill, the King of the Border Men*. In this serial, later made into a book, was the genesis of America's great myth of the Old Frontier. Buntline set the character, and Cody did his level best to live up to it. All of the many writers who later were to follow the Buffalo Bill trail merely elaborated the legend Buntline had invented, even to the ironic and horrible fiction that made of Bill a teetotaler and a Temperance advocate. Colonel Prentiss Ingraham wrote and rewrote the legend in no less than 203 paper-bound volumes, many of which are still in print.

Shortly after the first Buntline story appeared, a party of New Yorkers went west at the invitation of General Sheridan to have a buffalo hunt. Buffalo Bill was their guide. In the party was James Gordon Bennett the younger, the liveliest newspaper publisher of the time. Bennett was entranced with Buffalo Bill. He had never seen anything like this fine figure of a man, dressed in light buckskin that dripped with fringe, a crimson shirt and a fancy sombrero topping a head of magnificent hair that rippled down over his shoulders. His mustaches curled upward, and he wore a small goatee to complete the classic profile of what all American plainsmen were henceforth to look like. Buffalo Bill rode his snow-white horse with ease, and there was dash about his every move.

Bennett invited Cody to visit New York, and a bit later General Sheridan aided the scout in getting passes from the railroads. Bennett sent the scout $500 for travel expenses, and Cody took off. He stopped in Chicago long enough to purchase a dress suit; and was a little surprised and very happy to find himself already something of a hero, due to Buntline's earnest efforts. He was entertained at a number of dinners, then went to see Niagara Falls and so to New York.

Bennett met Cody and had him put up at the Union Club, where his yellow buckskins popped the eyes of both the staff and the members. He called on Buntline, who was living in style at the Brevoort, and learned that a play based on Buntline's Buffalo Bill stories was about to appear. While waiting for this event, Cody attended a stupendous dinner given in his honor in the August Belmont mansion by the great financier himself. On the next evening Bennett staged a big dinner for the scout, but Bill failed to show up and the disappointment was great. The next day he admitted to Bennett that he had somehow become "badly confused and demoralized," what with horsecars and cabs everywhere and a bar on every corner and several in between.

Then came the premier of *Buffalo Bill, the King of the Border Men*, made by Fred G. Meader from one of Buntline's epics. The play was produced in the Bowery Theater, with J. B. Studley impersonating Buffalo Bill. Bill himself sat in a box with Buntline to see one of the most extraordinary plays ever presented in New York. Chased by Indians, the hero crawled into a hollow log which lay in the very center of the stage. The redskins, alarmed by the mysterious disappearance of their intended victim, and apparently too stupid to inspect the log, sat down to hold council and make medicine. This called for a council fire and—well, it happened. The redskins built their fire against the log; and while the gallery gods sat forward breathless, the great scout was slowly being baked in the log oven. Just when the suspense was getting wholly beyond endurance, Buffalo Bill heaved his powderhorn into the flames, blowing the copper-skinned morons in all directions.

At the end of the play the spotlight was turned on the box, and the real Buffalo Bill got his first taste of the illumination that he was to love and cherish for the next forty years and more. But this time the light dazzled him and he could only mumble a few unintelligible words. The ovation, however, was deafening.

Always a generous soul, and feeling now that he should do

something in return for the honors and hospitality heaped upon him, Bill threw a big party at Delmonico's Restaurant. He had thought that the $50 he still possessed from the Bennett endowment would be sufficient for all expenses. It turned out he was short by several hundred dollars. Embarrassed and no little bemused at such expensive doings, he had to call for Buntline to settle the difference.

Bill soon started for the plains, stopping off between trains in Omaha, where friends insisted that he let them see how he looked in the claw-hammer suit and silk hat he had bought in the East. He put them on, and the party that followed was enthusiastic. Kind hands hoisted him aboard a westbound train, still wearing his dude clothes and weighted with a quart of rye in each hip pocket. Next afternoon he arrived, fragrant and none too steady, in the brilliant sunshine at Fort McPherson, appareled in all of his ballroom finery, his long hair tucked up under the topper. It was reckoned one of the great events in the old Army post's stirring history.

Cody quickly put away his Eastern clothes, got into buckskins, and went scouting for the Third Cavalry. On May 22, 1872, he was awarded the Congressional Medal of Honor for gallantry in action against the hostiles at Platte River, Nebraska. For the next forty-four years the Medal of Honor was Buffalo Bill's proudest possession, until February 15, 1917, when a churlish War Department removed the names of more than nine hundred Medal holders from the official list. Cody's was among them, though the removal of it was not the result of doubt that he had earned it. Cody came off the distinguished list simply because he had been neither an officer nor an enlisted man at the time it was bestowed. He had been a civilian scout and hence not eligible for the award. It was a cruel deed, to a man who in 1917 was old, with less than a year to live.

IV

Cody's scouting days were about over in '72; Ned Buntline was after him again. He wrote Cody letter after letter urging him to get into show business. He said he had written a fine play for him to act in. If Cody would come to Chicago, bringing along a dozen or so Indians, Buntline would produce a show that would take the big city on the lake by storm, and make Cody and Buntline a lot of money. Finally Cody could resist no longer. Taking with him a character known as Texas Jack, but forgetting all about the Indians, Cody arrived in Chicago on December 12, 1872. Buntline was disappointed to see no Indians; but he himself had forgotten something—forgotten to write the play. But that was nothing. Buntline first went out and rented a theater for $600 for one week, then sat down and in four hours wrote *Scouts of the Prairie*. Between Thursday and Monday night he rehearsed the cast, including ten dubious waterfront characters whom he had enticed to be Indians at twenty-five cents a performance.

The show opened on December 16. The ten Indians were killed, then rekilled in each act, and the audience thought it wonderful, even though a nasty drama critic wrote of the play that he wondered why Buntline had taken all of four hours to write it. The show pleased Chicago, then went to St. Louis, then to New York where it opened at Niblo's Garden for a long run. Buffalo Bill had come out of the world of literature and was now a handsome living god behind the footlights, where all could see and hear him.

After one season under Buntline's management, Bill thought his own share in the proceeds was too small. The next season he and Texas Jack opened their own show in New York. They talked Wild Bill Hickok, a renowned plains character, into playing a part, but soon found the truculent plainsman more than they could handle. It was bad enough when Wild Bill, irritated that the spotlight followed him across the stage, drew his Colt and shot the hell out of it. He insisted that the cold tea used in the play to simulate hard liquor be tossed out and the bottles filled with forty-rod. In the sham battles, Wild Bill, instead of shooting over the heads of the Indians, liked to shoot the blanks close to their bare legs, giving them powder burns. Buffalo Bill took him to task for this, and in the end Wild Bill went to his dressing room, got out of his stage clothes and left the theater, then and for all time, asking the stage carpenter to "tell that long-haired son-of-a-bitch I got no use for him or his show."

Wild Bill or no Wild Bill, Cody's second season as an actor was most successful, and he closed it "rolling in wealth." The show's success in this particular season, and in all subsequent seasons, was due in great part to the genius of Major John W. Burke, rated by those who saw him perform as the greatest press agent of all time.

Buffalo Bill's new public relations counsel wore his hair long and sometimes called himself Arizona John Burke. He hailed from Washington, D.C., and had been an actor and a newspaperman. He took firm hold of the Buffalo Bill legend where Buntline left off and blew it into the gigantic figure that I and all my generation remember from our youth. Burke really loved and revered Cody. In good times and bad, through all of the misfortunes that came to the show, largely because of Cody's love of liquor and women, plus his hazy ideas of business, Burke stood fast and never wavered.

Burke was welcome in every newspaper, railway and theatrical office in the United States. Everybody liked him, and though few believed his preposterous stories about Buffalo Bill and his show, they nevertheless printed them. They found him cars to move the show when other troupes could get no cars; and he could hire a theater out from under almost any contract. When scandal reared its head about Cody, Burke fetched up some new and wondrous incident in his hero's life and gave it to the world. Burke was also immensely popular with Indians, and he could do wonders with them and the government Indian Bureau.

While Buffalo Bill's show was touring the theaters, Cody met an actor and showman of great ability named Nat Salsbury, who told Cody that what he should have was an outdoor show, a tent show. Urged by Salsbury, Cody did start such a show, featuring himself and Gordon Lillie, known as Pawnee Bill. The show itself was fair, but it was badly managed, or rather not managed at all. "For the first five weeks out," Lillie said, "Cody was drunk every day." Salsbury saw the show and predicted it would soon fail. It did, and Cody went to Salsbury for help. Salsbury had a contract drawn up between himself, Cody and Captain A. H. Bogardus, "The World's Champion Pigeon Shot." The man who drew up the contract was John P. Altgeld of Chicago, later Governor of Illinois.

Under Salsbury's management and Major Burke's inspired press agentry, "Buffalo Bill's Original Wild West" was a success from the day it opened in 1884 until Cody's last public appearance in it in 1913. It toured the United States and Canada, then England, then Europe, playing, as the phrase has it, before the crowned heads of kingdoms and empires. Nat Salsbury proved to be one of the great outdoor showmen of the age, a man in Barnum's class. He and Burke were always thinking up new ways to startle the public. They took hold of Annie Oakley, five feet, one hundred pounds, nineteen and pretty, but unknown, and made her Little Sure Shot, the world's champion female with a rifle. Annie had ability to begin with. What she needed and what she got was special treatment from Burke's genius.

Old Sitting Bull, the surly Sioux, was advertised as having adopted Annie and she became, Burke swore, a member of the tribe and "a full Indian princess." Burke also attested to An-

nie's having broken 4,772 glass balls of 5,000 that were thrown
into the air. "How wonderful is this little miss from the Plains!"
he marveled in a thousand newspaper offices. At thirty paces
Annie would slice the thin edge of a playing card held toward
her. She shot dimes out of the air. She shot the ash off a cigaret
held in the lips of her husband, Frank E. Butler. Burke confided
to newspapermen that he had seen Annie shoot the spot out of
an ace of spades dropped from the top of the tent. In the proper
towns, and he knew which they were, Burke always told the press
that Annie's favorite reading was the New Testament. She remained with the show for most of seventeen years, dying in 1926
at the age of sixty-seven.

Among the many trials of Burke was Buffalo Bill's habit of
getting swacked at showtime, failing to hit the glass balls, even
with sizable charges of buckshot, and closing his performance
with a stump speech extolling the wonders of Kansas. Often when
he did this, the show happened to be playing in Massachusetts
or California. Burke tried to pass it off, saying it was due to Bill's
great and deep love for Kansas "where his much-beloved father
was the first to die in the struggle to free the slaves." In Boston,
Burke told the press Cody was "nine-tenths Irish, descended from
one of the early kings of Ireland." In Wisconsin, he remarked
that the original spelling of the great scout's name had been
"Koditz." In all of the towns and cities, Burke related how Buffalo
Bill had "avenged Custer's death" and, if urged in the least,
would go on to tell exactly how Cody had avenged the Battle of
Little Big Horn. No two versions agreed, but all of them appeared in the papers. Burke's stories, indeed, are the chief reason
why no reliable biography of Cody has ever appeared.

Work as he would, however, good John Burke could not dis-
sipate all of the scandalous rumors and charges about his ward,
for the Old Scout of the Plains was lusty and far from discreet.
The first time Gene Fowler interviewed Cody, he began by ask-

ing: "What did the duke really say, Colonel, when he caught you in the lady's room?" This referred to the well-known and probably true story concerning an English duchess with whom the gallant Cody had a liaison. But Cody was old then, and he refused to answer the brash young reporter's question.

v

At the turn of the century "Buffalo Bill's Original Wild West" was proceeding with the head of steam that carried it along even after Salsbury's death in 1902. But with Salsbury's going, both Buffalo Bill and the show started to disintegrate. Pawnee Bill bought into the show again and diluted it with his Far East features, thus producing what the aging though still imaginative Burke said was "a wedding of the Orient and Occident in gorgeous pageantry, pomp and procession." In Boston he told the *Transcript* man the new show was "a triumphal march of the ethnological congress." But something was lacking. In 1910 Bill announced that the season would be his farewell tour. They made a lot of money that year, and Cody put most of it into the several worthless gold and silver mines he had been supporting for years. In 1911 the show went out again, but to less business. In 1912 it was even worse.

It was getting time for the buzzards to gather. H. H. Tammen, an ex-barkeep who with a partner had set up as a newspaper publisher in Denver, loaned Cody $20,000 and took a mortgage on his portion of the "Wild West." Another clause in the instrument provided that Cody should leave his own show and appear in the Sells-Floto Circus, owned by Tammen. So in 1913 Buffalo Bill trouped in opposition to the show that still bore his name. Presently Tammen foreclosed on the "Wild West" and the outfit was sold by the sheriff. Tammen loaned more money to Cody and forced him to go out with the circus again. There followed a number of intricate deals, and when they were done

Buffalo Bill was merely a featured employee with Miller's "101 Ranch" show. Cody closed his show career with this outfit at Portsmouth, Virginia, on November 11, 1916. He had shattered his last glass ball.

When Fowler interviewed Buffalo Bill, the old man seemed to him a sad, lonely figure, his money gone, his show gone, the eyes of the United States no longer on the Old Frontier but on Europe, where slaughter on a gigantic scale was being done. A few months later Cody died, and his body was hardly cold when Mayor Robert W. Speer of Denver had a beautiful idea, one worthy of John Burke: Bill should be buried by the people of Denver on top of Colorado's Lookout Mountain, deep in the solid granite, with a funeral fit for a King of the Plains. North Platte, Nebraska, wanted the body for burial there, where Bill had a home. So did Cody, Wyoming, the town named for Bill and where he had lived. Denver had the body and Denver prevailed.

Denver embalmers used all their arts on the old hero while workmen blasted and drilled in the mountain wall. Thousands came on special trains for the orgy, and thousands trudged up the steep hill to the grave, among them six of Bill's surviving sweethearts. While the ceremonies were going forward, one of the six old girls rose from her camp chair with what Fowler, who watched fascinated, said was a manner so gracious and regal as to command respect. Then, as if she were alone with *her* dead, and while the vast audience gaped, the woman walked to the casket and held her antique black parasol over the glass in the coffin through which the still handsome face of the Prince of the Prairies peered. She stood there during the remainder of the long service, a fantastic and superb figure.

Denver soon began to realize what a truly stupendous attraction it had in the grave of Buffalo Bill. A million people visit the spot each year. In time, certain citizens of Wyoming threatened to dig up the body and move it where they thought it belonged—in Cody. Denver was alarmed, and presently fifteen tons of railroad iron and concrete were used to seal the grave.

Let Buffalo Bill's bones remain where they are, to mark a spot of pilgrimage for those who can remember the buckskinned god who sat his white horse so nonchalantly and shot the pretty balls into tinkling showers of glass, while a forty-two-piece band blared out *The Stars and Stripes Forever*. . . . It was a moment no American can forget.

A gilded chariot carried the novel into nonfiction-reading homes.

General Wallace and "Ben-Hur"

MOST literate Americans have read or at least heard of General Lew Wallace's tremendously popular *Ben-Hur: A Tale of the Christ* which appeared with little noise in 1880. The book seemed at first a dismal flop, but within a year its sale started to pick up and it has never ceased. Thirty-three years after its publication, a Chicago mail-order house purchased an edition of 1,000,000 copies—"each book covered with a jacket showing a gorgeous reproduction of the Chariot Race" —and sold them with little effort. *Ben-Hur* was translated into almost every language and was also one of the first novels to be put into "raised letters," as Braille used to be known.

What makes *Ben-Hur* historically important, however, is neither its wide popularity nor its theme. It is an epochal book because it was the first American novel to break through the rustic and village opposition to popular fiction. *Ben-Hur* rode that gilded chariot right through the front door to enter the homes of Hard-Shell Baptists and Methodists and other non-novel-reading sects, and to an eager welcome. Thousands of back-country Americans first learned the charms of fiction from *Ben-Hur*. *Uncle Tom's Cabin* doesn't count because it was not considered a novel at all but a Christian tract dictated by a Northern Congregational god.

The man who wrote *Ben-Hur* was as remarkable as his book, but all else about him, save this one volume, has largely been

Copyright, 1944, by Stewart H. Holbrook. Originally published in *The New York Times*.

forgotten. He was born Lewis Wallace at Brookville, Indiana, in 1827, the son of a distinguished father. Young Wallace was a restless youth who liked to hunt, to fish, play soldier, and also to write and paint. Before he left home to serve as an officer in the Mexican War he had finished a novel, *The Man at Arms: A Tale of the Tenth Century*. It was never published. He also started another story titled *The Fair God*, of which more later.

During the 1850's Wallace practiced law, was elected to the United States Senate, and moved his home to Crawfordsville, Indiana, where he devoted much time to drilling a militia company. At the outbreak of war in 1861 he was made adjutant general of the State and did a bang-up job recruiting Hoosiers and drilling them. He went to war himself and made a fine record, serving ably at Fort Donelson, at Shiloh, stopped the Confederate General Kirby-Smith in his attempt on Cincinnati, and held the formidable Jubal Early at bay in 1864 when the raider seemed about to take Washington.

Full of military honors, Wallace returned to Indiana after the war and completed the novel he had started many years before. *The Fair God* (1873) was quite a success, and its author at once began work on his magnum opus. It has often been related that Wallace was inspired to write *Ben-Hur* as a reply to the heretical utterances of Col. Robert Ingersoll, the noted agnostic. This story was doubtless manufactured as publicity pap to please those readers to whom the amiable Ingersoll was a horned devil. Wallace himself said his inspiration came from a passage in the New Testament: "Now, when Jesus was born in Bethlehem of Judea, in the days of Herod, the King, behold there came three wise men from the East to worship him."

He began writing *Ben-Hur* in 1875, with the idea of serial publication in a magazine. He put an immense amount of work into the background—studying and checking books of travels and travelers, comparing them with detailed maps, delving into geology and ethnology—writing slowly and constantly. He wrote as often as he could in the beech grove around his Crawfordsville home; but his law practice called for some attention, and he wrote at his book in his office, in courtrooms, in hotels. He composed Tirza's song, "Wait Not," on a belated train between Indianapolis and Crawfordsville. He worked best, he believed, beneath a favorite old beech tree.

"How often, when its thick branches have protected me with their cooling shadows, has it been the only witness to my struggles; and how often, too, has it maintained great dignity when it might have laughed at my discomfiture. The soft twittering of birds, the hum of bees, the lowing of the kine, all made this spot dear to me."

But he didn't finish the book under the beeches. Instead, the last chapter was done in "a vile old chamber" in the fort at Santa Fe, a "gloomy den indeed," where he found himself by grace of having been appointed Territorial Governor of New Mexico in 1878. Here he could not devote all his time to writing. Hell was popping. He had a feuding cattle war on his hands, and he also had William Bonney, worse known as Billy the Kid, a buck-toothed, adenoidal hoodlum who killed for the hell of it and is the hero of several dismal ballads.

Ben-Hur appeared in mid-1880. Very slowly it worked into a best seller. In thirteen years it had sold 600,000 copies. It reached the 1,000,000-copy mark about 1911. The House of Harper informs me that at least 2,500,000 copies have been sold. The exact figure cannot be known.

Ben-Hur made Wallace a national character, and in 1881 President Garfield appointed him Minister to Turkey, telling him: "General, I shall expect another book out of you," and added, "Your official duties will not be too numerous to allow you to write. Locate it in Constantinople." Thus did a President give an assignment to write a book. And the United States Government subsidized Wallace with a well-paid sabbatical that lasted four years. Wallace followed Garfield's suggestion, writing *The Prince of India,* a rather tiresome and long-winded tale with the Wandering Jew as a principal character. The book appeared in 1893 and did very well, though it never achieved the popularity of *Ben-Hur.*

Throughout his long life Wallace remained simple and democratic. Tall, erect and urbane, and fluent as well, he was a favorite, second only to Ingersoll, on the lecture platform. An interviewer wrote that Wallace was the most generous of his time in encouraging young writers. The late Will D. Howe, writer and editor, thought that Wallace's interviewer was possibly overly enthusiastic. Mr. Howe recalled Wallace, whom he knew, as a man who kept his eye pretty much on the ball, who was not prone to giving much time or thought to young writers of the day.

In spite of *Ben-Hur's* theme, Wallace was never a member of any church. He died in 1905, aged seventy-eight, a typical relic of the old school, still wearing his Custer-like mustaches, plus a beard in the Benjamin Harrison tradition.

There can be little doubt as to *Ben-Hur's* influence. Carl Van Doren, who was reared in a region where popular novels, in spite of the pure and prissy fiction of E. P. Roe and J. G. Holland, had never really been accepted, hands the palm to *Ben-Hur* and to *Ben-Hur* almost alone for breaking down the barriers of Hard-Shell Calvinism and letting American fiction into the homes of the pious pioneers of the Middle and Far West.

"Ben-Hur," says Mr. Van Doren, "positively won the ultimate victory over village opposition. It was read by thousands who had read no other novel except perhaps *Uncle Tom's Cabin,* and they hardly thought of either book as a novel. Still more thousands learned to know the geography, ethnology and customs of first-century Judea and Antioch as through no other source." Mr.

Van Doren also thinks that *Ben-Hur* contains "a vitality which has a touch of genius."

Many American missionaries and colporteurs were inspired to their work by *Ben-Hur*. One of the best of them, the bluff and able Albert L. Shelton, who spent so many years in China and Tibet, said flatly that the idea of becoming a missionary had never entered his head until his first reading of Wallace's book. Other missionaries translated *Ben-Hur* into Oriental languages.

The play, which William Young adapted from the book, increased *Ben-Hur's* fame and sales. On April 2, 1907, the stage version gave its 2,500th consecutive performance at New York's Academy of Music; and *Ben-Hur* road companies played every American city that could offer a theater with a stage large enough for the treadmill needed for "the Stupendous Chariot Race—Real Horses, Real Charioteers."

*The he-men beyond the mountains
get a working-over.*

Western Males Are Sissies

FOR close to a century we males of
the West have enjoyed the reputation of being astonishing he-
fellows—rough, tough, and lusty. It is still widely believed, east
of the Mississippi, that Westerners are all more than six feet
tall, except perhaps for a few weaklings who scale only five foot
eleven. I know mature but untraveled men in Boston and New
York who believe their Western brothers shoot off cigar ashes
with Colts, and in their lighter moments are given to demolish-
ing saloons.

These quaint opinions were formulated by the Deadeye Dick
school of writer, and they are being perpetuated currently in
books and magazines and movies by the heirs of old Deadeye.
The fiction formula runs thus: All Western males are not only
tall but handsome as the very devil, bronzed all over, with clear
if squinty eyes that reflect love of the hills and great open spaces;
they may be somewhat rough and hearty in their manners—
sometimes even given to windiness—but the hearts that pump
red and negative-Wassermann blood into Western arteries are
without guile. Honest guys to a man, and hard as nails.

But are Westerners like that? Are the slickers of the effete
East just a bunch of pansy-pickers compared to us of the great
plains and high mountains?

So far as pansy-pickers are concerned, we don't have many
pansies—the real flowers, I mean—in the West. We go in for

roses, tulips, cherry and orange blossoms, and things like that. Along about June every year, daily papers in California and the Pacific Northwest begin running pictures of males, some of them fat and well under six feet tall, twining roses in their hair or juggling tulips and olives or playing with sprays of cherry and orange blossoms. It's a sober fact, Western fiction to the contrary, that flowers play a large part in our he-Western lives. Tourists coming to the West Coast must often be amazed that the symbol of a well-known transcontinental train is a large pink cabbage rose. The Western terminus of this pretty train—the Portland Rose—is naturally enough Portland, Oregon, scene of many of the operations of the late and eminent Harry Tracy, the Lone Bandit, who was scarcely mighty lak a rose. Harry shot and killed seven men once, when he wanted a brief vacation from the Oregon pen, but that was long ago and Harry was a native of Wisconsin, anyway.

There's the city of Bellingham, Washington. Bellingham goes hog-wild about tulips every spring, and the he-men of town parade with armfuls of flowers. In Salem, capital of Oregon, the large, tough males prefer cherry blossoms and dance around the orchards with pretty sprays and get their pictures in the newsreels. In towns and cities all over northern California, the heirs of Black Bart and Joaquin Murietta make whoopee in the olive groves. (*In a flash Dick pulled his .45 and let go.*)

Those bullfrog jumping contests of the Mother Lode country have been revived out of a nostalgic and comical attempt at atavism—like the long hair affected by movie males—but miners have no hand in them and they serve chiefly to show off the new clothes of Hollywood cuties, both male and female. Cheyenne and Pendleton continue their "roundups" which are held solely to take money from more Hollywood cuties and from a swarm of wide-eyed tourists who fancy they are seeing a Wild West that actually exists.

Or take Idaho, where Big Bill Haywood used to range the hills and where dynamiting mines was the principal sport. That's he-country if ever there was any; Idaho sports are very fond of rude doings in the great outdoors. In a mountain valley they now have a million-dollar hotel, steam-heated, with warm swimming pools, and with electricity so that he-men can plug in their shavers; and when they do go outdoors a rope pulls the intrepid skiers all the long hard way up the mountain; the same mountain, by the way, up which prospectors walked with ninety pounds of pack on their backs. Branch shops of famous New York stores and dressmakers clutter the hotel. (*"She's th' purtiest gal in th' whole camp," Dick said.*)

It's all very he-Western.

The hunters are as tired as the skiers. Not for years has a Western store sold a ten-gauge shotgun—too heavy to lug around. And as for those incredible hunting seats—things that are strapped around the waists of hunters so that they may sit down without getting their pants wet—a Seattle store is reported to sell more of these contraptions than any firm in the United States. But neither hunting nor skiing is the true Western sport. The native Western man wants golf, and by God he gets it. Every vacant place in and around San Antonio, San Francisco, and Portland is taken up with links. The same is true of Boise, Reno, El Paso, and Spokane, the once-wild town Bing Crosby comes from. (*"We'll run him out of these parts," vowed the sheriff.*)

But golf is doubtless on the way out. It's too rough. Omaha, San Francisco, and Seattle have taken up badminton in a big way, and you can see feathered corks being batted around by the bronzed he-men whose grandpappies fought Indians for sport on weekdays and on Sundays played at hot-bottom, with a hickory whiffletree for a paddle.

Fishing, of course, never had a right to be called a he-sport, and it grows less-he yearly here in the West. Most fishermen carry enough poles and tackle and sleeping bags and cooking stoves and fly lotions and cocktail shakers to stock an emporium. I saw one party recently, on the wild Deschutes in Oregon, who had all these things plus a trailer and were bellyaching because the patent stove they had brought along wouldn't work. These Western fishermen even wait for state and federal agencies to tell them the probable weather and of the condition of the water in the streams they *may* fish—if it doesn't rain and the water isn't dangerously high and if the fish are reported hungry.

II

In urban parts of the West things are even softer than they are in the Western "wilds" into which sportsmen ride in their super-sixes and trailers equipped with indoor privies and dishwashing machines. In the cities symphony concerts, religious doings of one kind and another, and fruit, flower, and wheat festivals, occupy much of the time of the virile males. There is scarcely a city of any pretention that doesn't boast of an agate collectors' club and a philatelic society; and there is no Western town so backward that its newspaper does not carry a society page with pictures of bronzed Western males wearing shorts and engaged in the sinister pastime of racquets. . . . It would make Marcus Whitman and Gen. Custer and Collis P. Huntington roll fitfully in their graves.

We town guys of the Great West are very careful of our muscles. It wasn't for nothing that a Western man devised and put on the market a dingus to save Western he-men the trouble of stoking their furnaces. This highly successful automatic coal-stoker has saved the backs and arms of six-foot males for better things, like golf and chess and badminton. (*Dodging behind the bar, Dick crouched and pulled the trigger.*)

As for riding horses, only a few eccentric Westerners do that any more. The Western lumberjack runs his own car direct to camp, and a goodly share of the gaunt, tall and godlike cowboys ride herd in Fords that are rigged up with automatic starters and a radio, so that the bellowing of cattle is drowned out by the braying of a dance band from Miami. Year by year, legs in the old cowtowns are growing less bowed. The ancient cowboy yell sounds more like a soprano "yoo hoo." The old Barbary Coast of San Francisco is sinful no more but has gone chin whisker, its sidewalks and old dives piled high with eggplant, lettuce, and avocados, the favorite hearty food of Western men. (*"I could eat a hunk o' rawhide," bellowed hungry Deadeye Dick.*)

Maybe it is this sort of food that is responsible for our depressing record of prizefighters. Every little while we produce a new coming champ who goes East and is slapped down pronto by some broken palooka who has never been west of Brooklyn. Even our bloodhounds, once our pride, have gone sissy. About a year ago officers brought a famous pack from Walla Walla to Oregon, to run down an escaped convict. The hounds sniffed awhile, bayed once and led the posse direct to a cat and her kittens which were sleeping on a back porch in—of all places— Sweet Home, a village of Linn County. (*I'll git that man ef it takes to Judgment Day," snarled the ranger.*)

We still boast a few explorers and mountain climbers, but they go into the Great Alone well prepared. Last fall an old trapper on the Olympic Peninsula, coming into Hoh, Washington, for his winter supplies, reported that halfway up a mountainside in his region he had discovered a bushel of empty Sterno cans and a "long rubber bag, what you blowed up like a bicycle tire."

It is true that the West today swarms with writers of he-man Western stories, but they lead sheltered lives to a man, and they write solely of men long dead or of men who never lived anywhere at any time. Not one of them rolls his own cigarets, nor wears spurs. They belong to Rotary and Kiwanis, both estimable organizations but hardly he-male in the Western tradition. At least two of these writers use electric typewriters. (*The Kid's eyes squinted. "Bang, bang," he shot from the hip.*)

And there's tobacco. When pioneer merchants opened their stores on Puget Sound and San Francisco Bay they were hard put to keep enough plug-chewing in stock. Today a few pounds of chewing would supply the entire West for a week. Even cigarets are too strong; currently there is a big run on a device that is said to filter all the nasty nicotine out of cigarets, thus keeping the bronzed Western males from getting too dark-skinned.

As a final commentary there are the skidroads—or what are left of them. Skidroads are those parts of all Western cities where the hard-rock men, the loggers, the straw shovelers, the gaycats, and the dingbats congregate to make whoopee. In their heyday they supported places like the gigantic Erickson's, in Portland, and the immortal Paris House with its one hundred female inmates of all colors. The fun was rough and dangerous. Not long ago a manicure parlor was opened, especially for men, on Portland's notorious Burnside Street. A similar place is in operation on Butte's Silver Street, another on Yesler Way, in Seattle, named for Henry Yesler who could throw a five-pound ax sixty feet and hit a knothole.

Thus does the bronze on Western males fade. It is fading very rapidly, these past few years, and many of the males are less than the standard six feet tall. They hunt with a seat attached to their soft behinds; they fish from tiled trailers; they explore mountains with a pack of canned heat and a rubber mattress on their backs; they ride herd in automobiles. Few of them have ever fired a revolver. Their eyes still squint, not from looking at far mountains and blinding cactus deserts, but from searching for the little white ball that went off the fairway just below the clubhouse.

*The rabbit warren of the Hub of
the Universe is*

Boston's Scollay Square

THE visitor to Boston who does any casual strolling whatever is pretty sure to find himself in Scollay Square. He doesn't need to plan it so. He may even wish to avoid Scollay Square. But first thing he knows there he is in the middle of the most fearsome maze of streets, dead ends, rookeries, and rabbit warrens in all North America, a thing certainly of no beauty, but a wonder unique in cities of the United States. If Boston is the Hub of the Universe, then Scollay is the Hub of the Hub.

It is not given to man, even a Bostonian, to describe in anything like adequate terms the flavor of Scollay Square. A visitor might liken it to New York's Bowery, but if he did he would be no nearer the fact than if he likened it to the Place de la Concorde in Paris. True, it still musters a few employment offices, now fallen on hard times. It has garish penny arcades, burlesque theaters, cheap hotels, tattooing parlors, gaudy movie houses, and more often than not a drunk asleep in the gutter. But Scollay Square has something else; and this other element, this overlying flavor or characteristic, is the largely unseen yet powerful sense of old things, ancient things by American standards, many of them great and good things in the best sense, and as solidly American as corn meal and Medford rum. These press on Scollay Square from all sides, and Scollay has more sides than any other so-called square in the country, if not in the world.

113

Perhaps this indefinable feeling that inhabits Scollay lies in the realm of metaphysics, but it is as real as the cobblestones which have given kidney complaint to generations of drivers of herdics, coaches, and taxicabs. I am not given to undue whimsy, and never in my youth saw the shade of Dan'l Webster delivering an oration from the wrought-iron balcony of the Revere House of blessed memory. But if any reasonably sober man told me he had seen such a sight, I should readily believe him. Scollay exerts a potent influence. It is also the place where more men have become lost than in the Maine woods. One sees them occasionally, roaming aimlessly in attempts to discover the outlet from the Square that will lead them to the Parker House or to the North Station, gibbering, making motions, wildly gazing up at street signs which apparently conflict and give the direct lie to each other, until at last the lost stranger, no matter how determined, is driven to ask a cop or bootblack to lead him, shaken and twitching, to the sudden peace and quiet of King's Chapel Burying Ground, less than five rods from where he was standing when he gave up and demanded succor.

Scollay wasn't always thus. For the first fifty years of Boston's existence it was a pasture, wherein the cows, true to bovine folkways, made winding paths. Then, before 1684, a schoolhouse was erected here, "against Captain Samuel Sewall's house." In 1753 the school was enlarged, and Samuel Holbrook made schoolmaster at an annual salary of £60. In 1790 this school was abandoned and William Scollay bought the building. This Scollay was the son of John, a selectman of Boston, and William was also prominent, for his name appears on the cornerstone of the new State House, laid July 4, 1795, as the Right Worshipful Master of a Masonic lodge. William also bought a row of buildings next to the schoolhouse, living in one of them and renting the others. They became known as the Scollay Buildings and were occupied for years by barbers, braziers, lawyers, and the largest tea store in the city.

In 1816 the old school building and other structures in the area were torn down to make a new street, Cornhill, and the Scollays received an indemnity. By this time scores of wood or brick buildings had risen beside the crooked cowpaths. Lawyers still infested them, and in one was the office of Frank Gleason, who brought out the first pictorial newspaper in America. In 1838 the area officially became known as Scollay Square. Stages used it as a terminus, and a bit later it was the end of the line for the Middlesex (horsecar) Railroad.

II

In the early 1840's the followers of William Miller, the prophet of Doomsday, acquired a lot on Howard Street, leading to the Square, and erected their temple as a refuge for the chosen at the end of the world, which appeared imminent every little while until 1845. The temple then became a theater which has just now completed its one hundred and second season as the Old Howard. Large hotels went up, the American House in 1835, the Quincy, the Crawford, the Revere following. (The Revere House was on Bowdoin Square, at one time distinct from though adjacent to Scollay, but today no man can say where Scollay leaves off and Bowdoin begins.) To these hotels, then the finest in New England, came the great of the nation, where they rode, in the Crawford, in what is said to have been the first passenger elevator in the country; and enjoyed at the Revere House its high, wide rooms and notable hospitality— people like the Grand Duke Alexis; the Prince of Wales (Edward VII); the singers Patti, Titjens, and Nilsson; Presidents Pierce and Fillmore; and the great Webster himself, reckoned by most Yankees of the time as their most eminent man, and jovial, too, especially so at the Revere House where the punch was stout and the tumblers large.

Facing Scollay Square from the upper side for half a century was Austin & Stone's Museum, an institution to be compared favorably with Plymouth Rock and Bunker Hill Monument. It combined variety shows with an ever-changing Congress of Freaks, of whom Karmi, the Sword Swallower, still lives (1948) in near-by Malden. No country boy come to Boston missed Austin & Stone's. Over the entrance to this place was a small coop wherein sat three musicians who for thirty-eight years drank one beer or whiskey on the hour and half-hour and played the same tune over and over. I had the great honor once to buy one of these artists a beer. He was a small, moth-eaten man, fragrant of hops and rye, and he told me that in twenty-two years neither the personnel of the three-piece band nor its one-piece repertoire had undergone a change. Today no one seems to recall what that one tune was, but all agree that it was never heard elsewhere. I asked this musician about the show in Austin & Stone's, but he said he had never seen it.

The indisputable genius of Austin & Stone's was Professor William S. Hutchings (1832–1911), a man of small stature but of vast powers and great dignity. He was the Lecturer, coming to that height by way of Barnum & Bailey, for whom he had been the Boy Lightning Calculator. The Professor's lectures on the freaks on view at Austin & Stone's were wonders of polish, erudition, and grave amazement. Nine times a day, six days a week, he lectured on ten different freaks, and to hear him was to marvel. Students of forensic at Harvard were urged by their professors to listen to Professor Hutchings, and none needed urging who once came within range of his powerful though cultured voice. "Now for the Ossified Man," the Professor would remark. "The Ossified Man. Os is from the Latin. Os means bone. Full of bones. Full of bones. The Latin is dead, but the

Ossified Man still lives. O, God, 'tis wonderful, wonderful!"
Frank Buxton (Harvard 1900), later editor of the *Boston
Herald*, recalls that the Professor's calling on Deity to witness
the wonders of the Museum was done with such reverence as
never to shock the mores of the customers. And when he came
to the Egyptian Chess Player, the Professor opened up with
everything, and before he was done the gaping yokels from
Lakeport, New Hampshire, and Mattawaumkeag, Maine, had received a solid grounding not only in the history of chess, but
also in the history of Egypt, its rulers, philosophy and customs,
punctuated at proper intervals by the pounding of the Professor's gold-headed cane.

Across the Square from Austin & Stone's was the Nickelodeon,
perhaps the first so named in this country. Here for five cents
one saw a variety show, but it never developed remarkable characters like Professor Hutchings. Waldron's Casino, once home
of wheel burlesque, now plays Italian language movies—or did
until recently; and the Bowdoin Square Theater, where Dave
Marion, Sliding Billy Watson, and Al Reeves once cavorted, also
has been reduced to movies. The ancient Crawford House still
stands, dingy and weatherbeaten, but doing very well with a
night club.

III

Standing in Scollay Square today one can walk a few rods in
any direction and come square into antiquity, or history. Along
the brief course of Cornhill (to which "street" is never ap-
pended) are secondhand bookshops, notable among them Coles-
worthy's, established in 1837 and still in the same family. Next
door is the Phoenix Coffee Mills where, if one is prepared to
stand and not sit, one can drink the best cup of coffee in town.
The Phoenix has been serving coffee for almost one hundred
years.

A few steps down Tremont, one immediately drops out of the hurdy-gurdy of Scollay and faces squat, black old King's Chapel, whose bell, by Revere, has a deep and haunting voice, and the Chapel Burying Ground, where lie the remains of the Colonial Governors Winthrop and Endecott, and those of William Dawes, he who rode that night with Revere but had no immortalizing agent like Longfellow. A few feet away is Tremont Temple, where everyone from Methodist bishops to Joe Knowles, the old Nature Man, has held forth. Across Tremont is the Old Granary Burying Ground, where sleep the so-called martyrs of the so-called Boston Massacre. Paul Revere rests there, too, and so does the man who planned and agitated the Revolution—Samuel Adams. On the next corner, locally known as Brimstone, is Park Street Church.

Or, walk up the slope from Scollay. Here on the back side of Beacon Hill, much of it once the farm of the great John Cotton, is an amazing variety of things: the staid office of Calumet & Hecla, whose genius was Alexander Agassiz; Ford Hall; the Boston City Club; and the Swedenborgian Society with its startling sign, HEAVEN & HELL. Down hill are Bulfinch Street and Bulfinch Place, on one of which used to stand two stone dogs on guard at the front of what generations of Harvard men knew as a place of ill repute and excellent entertainment. In this area the old William Tell House still stands, a stopping place for theatrical people since the days of James K. Hackett's father. Here too is Bulfinch Place Chapel, "In the West End 119 Years." Where Bulfinch Street emerges to the Square—here technically Bowdoin Square—is the new Telephone Building, embedded in its side a bronze plaque to one of the city's most illustrious citizens of all time, Charles Bulfinch, the architect, whose home stood here.

Great preaching has been heard in these parts, too. A few steps down Brattle Street stood the Brattle Square Church, organized in 1665, where later preached such men as Edward Everett and John G. Palfrey, great names in New England still. During the siege of Boston (1775–1776) a cannon ball heaved from Cambridge by Colonel Knox's artillery bedded in the side of Brattle Square Church and there it remained until 1871, when the structure was razed.

Down the murky reaches of the preposterously designated Franklin Avenue—exactly 9 feet 6 inches wide, over-all—was the office of the *New England Courant,* James Franklin, Prop., whose brother Ben was printer's devil. Near-by was the office of Eades & Gill, printers, where met the Tea-Party Men to don their disguises.

One side of Scollay Square is Court Street, once Prison Lane, where the colonial lockup stood. Captain Kidd peered through its bars to watch Scollay's cows and city-rustics in 1699, and Hawthorne described the gaol in *The Scarlet Letter.* In 1836 five pairs of horses champed their bits and sixty-five yoke of oxen chewed their cuds, after delivering to the Square (at two to the load) the huge columns of granite they had hauled overland from Quincy for the new Court House. It must have made one of the great scenes Scollay has witnessed. Through this street hurried the mobs in a vain attempt to rescue Anthony Burns, Negro, from the slave catchers, and Thomas Wentworth Higginson, Theodore Parker, Wendell Phillips and others were arrested and charged with "obstructing the process of the United States." Other mobs ran through the Square to Faneuil Hall, less than a stone's throw, to listen while "a Gentleman in a Red Wig," who was probably Samuel Adams, gave an incendiary harangue, then proceeded to the Old State House and the Boston Massacre. For more years than men can remember the Ancient & Honorable Artillery Company paraded through Scollay from their headquarters in Faneuil Hall, from the cupola of which the famous grasshopper weathervane of Deacon Shem Drowne still marks the winds.

It was through Scollay that Dr. Parkman walked, with his long and quick strides, on that fatal day in 1849, on his way to Harvard Medical College, to see Professor Webster. The Professor was ready for him, that day, too, and Dr. Parkman hasn't been seen since, although the Professor was hanged for murder and went into history as the only murderer to perform while a member of Harvard College Faculty.

IV

The character of Scollay Square changed slowly until 1903, when things sort of went to pieces. In that year the bronze statue of Governor John Winthrop, the work of Richard S. Greenough, was removed from the Square because of congested traffic conditions and work on the East Boston Tunnel. Newer hotels and theaters and shops drew citizens and visitors farther south. The Revere, American, Crawford and Quincy Houses (all hotels) became second-rate. Pawnshops and employment offices moved into the Square, and there they remain, along with passport photo places, ten-cent hamburger joints, shooting galleries, slum-jewelry joints, aromatic eating dives and saloons, display windows of trusses, signs of doctors asking "Why Wear a Truss?", tattooing parlors ("See Dad Upstairs"), two-pants clothing stores—and noise. The noise comes from what are doubtless the roughest cobblestones in all geology, bumping the trucks and drays and cabs which weave and bounce through the Square in endless procession, day and night; from the rumble of subway trains; from the loudest penny arcades ever heard; from street hawkers and newsboys whose A's are broad and voices terrific; from Salvation Army bands and their sweet evangels.

Still looking down onto the Square are many buildings which have known better days and seen better things than the present. In spite of the shoddy present, these old structures made of eighteenth century brick retain a dignity, an aloofness, a staid old-timeness that is sure to strike the reflective visitor or citizen, especially at high noon, each weekday, when the deep, mellow peals of P. Revere's masterpiece announce that King's Chapel belfry remains the same, no matter what has happened to Scollay Square.

*ever mentioned by local boosters
is the Old Howard,*

Boston's Temple of Burlesque

BEACON HILL and Back Bay no longer patronize Boston's odd and ancient place of entertainment known as the Old Howard. It doesn't rate a line in any of the Chamber of Commerce's booklets on the city. This seems strange in a town that cherishes its other venerable institutions so highly, for the Old Howard is hoary with age and tradition, having enjoyed over one hundred consecutive seasons as a playhouse. Indeed, it is likely the oldest theater in the United States. And regardless of the aloof attitude of Boston's upper crust, the Old Howard is visited by more people every year than see Bunker Hill Monument and Faneuil Hall combined.

One approaches 34 Howard Street from Scollay Square, with its rumble of subway and litter of cheap hotels, penny arcades, saloons and shooting galleries. Howard Street is so narrow and usually so crowded that it is difficult to get a good view of the Gothic stone pile that rears up so surprisingly, its arched front presenting monstrous stained glass windows, three stories high, in this rabbit warren. Nor is there anything phony about the stone. It is granite, three feet thick, the same stuff that built Bunker Hill Monument. The Howard was built to last, and last it has in spite of the Watch and Ward Society, the attempted encroachments of civic enterprise and the changing habits of theatergoers.

During the past half-century local divines have applied terms
to the Old Howard ranging from "sink of sin" to "social can-
cer." The Watch and Ward Society has hauled its managers and
performers to jail. The Howard's management complains only
perfunctorily. Such "moral" hubbub is good for business, and
so are the many lewd stories circulated regarding the utter
depravity of the shows on the Howard stage.

There is a virtual school of this fiction in New England. In
the farthest reaches, such as Madawaska, Maine, and Columbia
Bridge, New Hampshire, I've heard the one about the female
dancer in tights at the Howard who was responsible for "grandfather being killed in the rush." I imagine this one has been
related as God's truth in the ports of the world.

No rural Yankee in my time, or in my father's time, had seen
Boston until he had furtively witnessed a performance at the
Old Howard. It was the same at Harvard, and graduates of that
university like to relate how the eminent John Fiske, the great
philosopher, used to remark that the Harvard curriculum included "Howard Athenaeum I, II, III and IV." A similar remark has been attributed by later generations of students to
Charles Townsend Copeland, to Albert Bushnell Hart, and to
practically every other well-known professor except Bliss Perry.
No seafaring man who ever made the port of Boston went away
without paying a visit to 34 Howard Street. No drummer missed
it, and there is ample reason to believe that no out-of-town parson
missed it either.

This word of mouth advertising for many generations is what
has filled the fifteen hundred Howard seats almost every afternoon and night since the place started going low-brow approximately sixty years ago. Before that, it had been the Howard
Athenaeum, a proud playhouse, one of Boston's finest.

And before that, it had been the exact place selected for the
physical ascension to heaven of the host of followers of William

Miller, the Millennial Prophet. No theater in America has had so implausible a beginning, nor so odd a career.

II

On the fearful 23rd of April, 1843, many thousands of weak-minded people in the United States gathered at previously selected places to greet the Last Day. This was to be no abstract matter, but a literal end of the world, the day of Jubilee, when all on earth except the sanctified were to be destroyed in a holocaust of fire. Gabriel was to wind his horn. The graves would yawn. And Christ Almighty would walk among his saved ones.

This interesting state of affairs was being brought about by the aforementioned William Miller, one of Vermont's many gifts to the nation, who had spent much of his life in a study of the biblical Revelation and in calculation of dates founded thereon. He finally came up with April 23, 1843, as the end of things. Had it not been for several go-getting pastors in Boston and New York City, the affair might never have gone farther than Miller's own rural community, but these men got hold of Miller's coat-tails and urged him on, meanwhile publishing a red-hot paper characteristically titled *The Midnight Cry*, and distributing luridly colored charts showing Prophet Miller's calculations and some of the damnedest seven-horned beasts ever imagined.

The effect on thousands of people in New England, New York and other Eastern communities was terrible to behold. Men and women gave away their farms, their houses, everything, keeping only enough white cloth to make ascension robes for the Last Day. They gathered in tabernacles everywhere, discussing the coming event, praying loudly, speaking in tongues, groaning, rolling, shouting, weeping.

Boston harbored thousands of these dim-witted folk. They bought a piece of pasture land on the lane that became Howard

Street and there erected a mighty tabernacle. Its interior was decorated, says an old account, with murals depicting the monsters in Revelation, things such as never were seen outside the realm of alcoholic hallucinosis. "No less horrible," says this contemporary account, "were the faces of the frenzied devotees who crowded the tabernacle for the Last Day. They waited for they knew not what and shrieked in agony, tearing their robes in frenzy. Many went stark mad."

All Boston was in ferment, the Millerites waiting the world's doom and their own salvation, the nonbelievers scoffing. Miss Clara Endicott Sears, author of the fascinating *Days of Delusion,* a serious study of the whole affair, reports that the scoffers gathered by the thousands on Boston Common on that fateful day to watch the Millerites ascend. It was thought they would probably rise straight up through the tabernacle's roof, and thence on to Heaven.

Prophet Miller, however, had made a miscalculation. He made subsequent miscalculations. The Trumpet never sounded. This left the Millerites to return to practical living, and the more businesslike of them proceeded to lease the Boston tabernacle to a theatrical company. The building was now disguised by a massive granite façade. The first play, given October 13, 1845, was Sheridan's *School for Scandal,* which incidentally had been the bill presented at Boston's first theater in 1792, when the play was broken up by the sheriff and the actors carted off to jail, charged with "a serious crime."

But no trouble marred the première at the Howard Athenaeum. For the next several months the place was filled nightly with delighted audiences, and things went fine and dandy until the evening of February 23, 1846. The play was *Pizarro,* and its climax was the descent of a ball of fire from the clouds. The ball duly descended from the flies, set the place afire, and destroyed it. No one was injured.

The site was empty, except for the granite wall, in the spring of 1846, and was taken over for a few weeks by a circus. Later that year the lot was purchased by Messrs. Boyd and Beard, who had an idea. They built a combined brewery and theater, using the gigantic blocks of granite already on the ground and more of the same. Whether this structure was made in Gothic form because the granite blocks already present formed the dominant arch, or whether the brewer-showmen sardonically followed the lead of Prophet Miller is not now clear. What is clear is that the building took on the form and likeness of a church which it has to this day.

Opening the new Howard Athenaeum was James H. Hackett, father of James K., and his company, in *The Rivals*, Mr. Hackett playing Sir Anthony Absolute. Patrons found they had to walk upstairs one flight to get to the orchestra (just as they do today) because the brewers needed the ground floor for their operations in ale. Patrons also found "a truly elegant playhouse." The orchestra was surrounded by sharply rising tiers of seats. Three tiers of boxes rose one above the other, all fancy with castiron grillwork, and whitewashed. Three horseshoe balconies rose to the ceiling, from the center of which hung a gigantic gaslight.

The Howard was now set for a quarter of a century of the carriage trade. English opera came. So did Italian. Matilda Heron, who first played Camille in the United States, was a sensation. The distinguished Mr. and Mrs. Charles Kean played several engagements. Junius Brutus Booth had a season. So did his hammy son, John Wilkes. Great attention was paid to staging and props. A drama of the chemically-minded Borgias presented in its third act a stage on which appeared thirty-eight coffins. Shakespeare held the boards off and on during the 1850–1870 period. The beautiful if overrated Lola Montez did her Spider Dance here.

Cora Mowatt and E. L. Davenport had engagements. So did Charlotte Cushman, and the eminent Macready himself.

Sometime in the 1870's the Howard's tone began dropping, and business grew better. John B. Stetson, a noted showman of the time, took over as manager, and he wowed 'em right off by booking what appears to have been the first Human Fly. This lad astounded Boston by walking around on the high ceiling of the Howard, meanwhile making cracks about the baldheads in the pit.

Manager Stetson believed in vaudeville, then called variety. He brought Tony Pastor and company to the Howard, and followed that sterling comic with a long line of comedians, singers, sword swallowers, fire eaters, and trained horses. He often staged a boxing "exhibition," and it was here that young John Lawrence Sullivan first attracted attention by nearly killing the great Professor Mike Donovan. Stetson also believed in burlesque, and presently Ida Simmons was offering *A Strike in the Harem, with Sixteen Beautiful Young Ladies in a Grand March.*

Manager Stetson was also an aesthete. He ordered his theater programs printed on purple paper, and I mean purple. He interlarded things like Miss Simmons' cuties with melodrama. In those days melodrama took some doing. Consider the bill at the Howard in January, 1883. It was *A Dark Secret*, and the posters announced it to be "a thrilling tale of the Thames Valley, with Marvellous Aquatic Scenes—the Henley Regatta, presented with Real Sailboats, Rowboats, Racing Shells and Steam Launches, the Stage Being Flooded with 5,000 Cubic Feet of Water."

Kate Fisher came in 1886 to play in *Mazeppa*, during which she was strapped to the back of a horse by the villain and underwent untold miles of plungings as the beast clop-clopped on the treadmill. Colonel Cody followed with a thrilling drama of the West titled *Twenty Days, or Buffalo Bill's Pledge*.

It was during this era that the purple programs of the Howard

began to carry a direct invitation to "Come Where the Woodbine Twineth," which was right next door at 19 Howard Street.
This was of course a saloon, and it advertised that "The Brass
Gong in our Refectory sounds two minutes before the Curtain
goes up on the Next Act." This would permit a serious drinker
time for at least one more ale. (Incidentally, the yeasty smells
that wafted into the Howard from the brewery became so powerful that the ventilating system had to be renovated several
times.)

III

When G. E. Lothrop took over the Howard in the early nineties, he stopped the old house custom of giving out seat checks
to patrons who wanted a drink between acts. The management
of the woodbine place, as well as other saloonkeepers in the
neighborhood, called on Mr. Lothrop in a body and protested.
Lothrop held fast—for one night. On that night, just when the
Howard's curtain went up on the first act, a ten-piece band, composed mostly of cornets and bass drums, took up position right
in front of the theater and let loose. Theater patrons couldn't
hear a word from the stage. On the next night, and ever thereafter, door checks were given out to thirsty patrons of the Old
Howard, as it was now coming to be known.

What might be called the Third, or Burlesque, Era of the Old
Howard began in the nineties. Weber and Fields played the
house, and so did a wide variety of performers, like Maggie
Cline, Gus Williams, Pat Rooney and Sam Bernard. It was from
the Howard's stage that John L. Sullivan, by then heavyweight
champion of the world, first invited all comers to stay four
rounds with him. He later appeared here in his great melodrama, *Honest Hearts and Willing Hands,* and told a reporter
he hoped someday to be as great an actor as Booth or McCul-
lough. "I've just started now," he said.

I got my first look at John L. at the Howard, and along with John for good measure, were Dainty Violet Mascotte and Her Thirty Merry Maids. Miss Mascotte and her company were a standard summer attraction at the Howard for many years. I remember them with the greatest pleasure.

A change came over the Howard's advertising. Once it had been dignified, a simple announcement of the coming bill, but now it fell almost as low as modern movie advertising. A sample:

You Boys in the Know will Get a Wallop out of Violet Mascotte and Her Merry Maids, Thirty, Count Them; Lovely, Lively, Artery-Softeners. Good for That Tired Feeling, With their Bear Skins, and Oh, My! But a Word to the Wise is Enough, and the Wisenheimers know There is Always Something Doing at the Old Howard from 1 to 11.

That final line about Always Something Doing has been the theme song in every Old Howard advertisement for more than forty years. It and the slangy copy were the work of Fred Doherty, long-time press agent for the house, who wrote every line of the copy until illness prevented. One may contrast it with the two-line couplet used in the fifties and sixties:

> As Rome points proudly to her Coliseum,
> So Boston treats her Howard Athenaeum.

But it is burlesque, with movies between shows, that has kept the Old Howard running these last four decades. Whether it is "worse" burlesque than is to be seen elsewhere is a matter of opinion. On occasion, Boston's Watch and Ward has said it was "positively rotten." In January, 1933, this group prevailed on the city fathers to close the Howard for thirty days. At the hearing Investigator Slaymaker for the W. and W. testified as to the "voluptuous dancing and profane dialogue" of the performers.

Mayor Curley, an old patron of the Howard, asked the agent if he could perform in a voluptuous manner. The agent said he could not. Attorney Whitman for the theater said that the Old

Howard was not supposed to be a young ladies' finishing school and that the Old Howard's patrons were able to take care of themselves, including their morals. Investigator Hill of the Society mentioned the "diaphanous brassieres" of the chorus, and the "mobile abdomen" of one of the star performers. He said the Howard was "worse than anything in Havana."

The hearing made a big uproar. For the first time in eighty-seven years the Howard was dark for thirty days in a theater season. Whether or not the house reformed is an abstract matter, but it is on record that it reopened with a bill called *Scrambled Legs*.

A bit later it appeared that at least a part of the Howard would have to be torn down, through condemnation proceedings, to permit erection of the new Suffolk County Court House. The new building went up, however, without injury to the old theater. That, plus a little labor trouble—no more than other theaters have had—was the last real menace the Old Howard has had to face.

Burlesque that *is* burlesque is what has kept the ancient and grimy joint busy now for half a century, and it still flourishes. On many nights, when the house is filled to the rafters and the strip-tease artiste gets down to the G-string, the shouts and cries that echo to the high ceiling might remind Prophet Miller of the great workings of the spirit when Gabriel was getting up a lip to blow that horn.

The Minskys may come and go. So may the Balaban & Katzes. But there is today, as almost continuously since 1845, always something doing from one to eleven at the Old Howard.

One of the great glories of Beacon
Hill is Louisburg Square.

Boston Nocturne

SOME hold that the Square looks its
best in winter, and at early candlelighting, when yellow beams
through the handsome bow windows pattern the snow, and the
figure of Aristides at one end of the oval green stands ghostly
in the twilight. I think it matters little. By sun or moon, in spring
or winter, the tiny piece of ground on the west slope of Beacon
Hill has more mellow charm than any other spot I know in the
United States. For well over a century it has been Louisburg
Square.

The moon must rise high over Boston Harbor before its rays
fall into the Square; and something happens to its beams, and to
those of the sun as well, when they touch the ancient houses and
the greensward caged in its fence of hand-wrought iron; the resulting lights and shadows are not to be caught on a lens but are
to be seen only in old prints.

The first thing that strikes one about the Square, after sensing
immediately its nostalgic beauty, is its serene aloofness, its
isolation. Here it is, almost in the heart of a great and crowded
city. Scarce a block away in every direction are arteries of tremendous traffic, and all around it Boston rumbles and bleats
and toots and clatters—yet here all of the noises are muted. The
roar of trucks on Charles Street arrives in the Square like the
murmur of a distant waterfall. Fire sirens along Arlington Street
would not rouse a dozing robin in the yews of the Square. And

the frightful din of the El's shuttle trains from North to South Stations sounds like a soft-footed maid pattering down a McIntire stairway. Indeed, for all I know, Louisburg Square may be the opposite of a sound pocket, if there is such a thing—a place that simply refuses to catch or even to listen to strident sound.

Doubtless the buildings that line the upper and lower sides have something to do with the seldom broken silence. They rise four, and some of them five, stories and form solid banks of brick and stone that shatter and repulse the dreadful noises of a modern city. At each end of the Square more solid houses on Pinckney and Mount Vernon Streets add to the wall of insulation Whatever the reason, one thing is certain: one steps from Boston and clamor into Louisburg Square and hush, in a matter of seconds.

One comes to the Square from any direction, but comes best, perhaps, by starting at Beacon and Tremont Streets, in the shadow of black old King's Chapel and the Parker House, both venerable institutions in the Hub of the Universe, and walking up Beacon Street, passing the cloistered Atheneum, passing Goodspeed's Book Shop, and the Capitol with its authentic Bulfinch wing, turning right to Mount Vernon Street, and so on over the brow of the Hill to the Square.

The Proprietors of the Square shall be held responsible for clearing the streets of snow, or debris of storms; and for all repairs and maintenance of the walks, the park, and its fence.

In a way the Square is no part of Boston at all, for this oval park, the streets and the sidewalks, all are privately owned and most privately administered by the Proprietors of Louisburg Square, one of the more hoary corporations of the city, who meet each February in a strictly private town-meeting to assess themselves for maintenance and to elect officers for the ensuing year. Lest the outland heathen mistakenly think this to be mere flum-

mery growing out of tradition, he should know that the City of
Boston, in a misguided moment, once erected a small polling
booth in the Square to be used in a municipal election. The Proprietors said nothing, but they sent an austere bill to the City
for rent amounting to $125, and the City paid.

Nor is an automobile to be parked here unless it is visibly
and genteelly sponsored by a special parking tag issued by one
of the Louisburg Square Proprietors. The Square, I repeat, is
private property and nowhere else on earth is private property
held in more esteem than in Louisburg Square.

*And they found himme, the said Wm. Blaxton, living alone
on ye hill above ye sea, the onlie white person in all this greate
solitude & Savage Wilderness. Yet ye same had huge store of
fruits & of bookes.*

I never fail to visit the place when I am in Boston. I like best
to walk it on a night in autumn and to reflect on its genealogy,
which is impeccable and goes back beyond the lines of come-
latelys like the Saltonstalls and Cabots, even beyond the Winthrops. Here when the leaves are falling and rustling across
the red bricks and whispering of winter coming down from New
Hampshire, I like to think of the Square's first proprietor, William Blackstone, who was an old settler when the Puritans arrived. They found him, did the Winthrops and Dudleys and
Mathers, the one white man in all these woods, an orchard already bearing behind his hut, his shelves stacked with some two
hundred well-read volumes.

There is yet a good deal of mystery about old Blackstone, this
primordial Bostonian. He was a genuine recluse who, if he must
have company, preferred "ye Indeans" to whites. In the midst
of his orchard he had dug a wondrous spring, a font that flowed
liquid ice throughout the year and fathered a small stream. He
himself was as cool as the spring to the Puritans, though he did

give them good aid and succor in their many troubles. He observed aloud that he had left England because of the lord-bishops, and now, he continued, he thought he did not like the lord-brethren any better. So, he presently pulled his stakes and went away, to make another lonely pitch on the heretical soil of Rhode Island, the only safe spot in all New Canaan for a man who strained at theological boundaries.

The acres of Blackstone on the Hill were handed down from one Puritan to another until, in 1769, they were purchased by John Singleton Copley.

Aye, a great genealogy, that of the Square. When he bought the land on the Hill, Copley was already one of Boston's most noted citizens, and rightly so, for his portraits of Otis and Revere and Samuel Adams and other stout Revolutionary Fathers are alive and magnificent, let the Modernists say what they will. Copley built him a fine house on Copley's Acres, a block from the present Square, and I can picture him coming here to gather the Blackstone apples and to lift a jug of pure cold water from the Blackstone spring, his fine hands stained from the pigments he used to paint the Patriots. But the shot that went around the world found the artist abroad and he never returned.

After the Revolution Copley's Acres was broken up and sold in pieces; and by 1820 that portion of it that is now the Square had begun to take on its present form, but not yet its name. That had to wait until 1834. It seems odd, and it would be odd in any other place but Boston, that the celebrated expedition against Cape Breton Island and Louisburg had been almost a century in the past before someone was inspired to immortalize it in name.

Many elegant domiciles were established in this place, which has just been named in honor of the intrepid Expedition led in 1746 by Sir William Pepperell against the French.

Sir William himself, scarlet coat and all, had been in his grave seventy-five years before the Square was named. But if it had to wait long for its christening, its glory was soon to come and its glory was no sudden blooming that withered swiftly. It was a long flowering that is yet, a century and more later, not in the sere. Neither Concord nor Cambridge was to know a greater intellectual and artistic era than that of the Square.

Miss L. M. Alcott, and her venerable father who is ailing, have lately moved into the house at Number 10 Louisburg Square.

Yes, that is the very same house. The numbers have not been changed. You should have seen the Square when Miss Alcott lived here. Unseemly street urchins took to haunting the place, to watch for the black carriage of the tall spinster who was usually wrapped in furs, even in August, to fight for first chance to open the door for her. Louisa May never failed to give them pennies, and often wiped a small nose with a dimity handkerchief that smelled of lavender. "Msalkot" was a goddess to these youngsters. They felt bad to see her shiver so, even when the sun was hot on the Square, and they felt worse when she coughed.

In her low, hoarse voice, Louisa May would often call them to this very door of Number 10, to give them some grapes or dessert that old Bronson, babbling his senility in an upper room, had refused. They knew she was some sort of writer, but they couldn't know that she wrote what she said was Moral Pap for the young. Yet it paid the interminable debts of her noble and incompetent father until, one day in March of 1888, at last—and talking still—he died. And poor Miss Alcott died two days after. . . .

There were other notables. Take Number 5 there, classic from its lowest step to the roof. In Number 5 the Honorable John Gorham Palfrey edited manuscripts for the *North American Review*, and he also wrote history and served in Congress. At the trial of an unfortunate Harvard professor, charged with applying a club to one of the Parkmans, Mr. Palfrey declared sonorously that Professor Webster was a man of some temper but of extremely good heart. . . .

The Square was saddened by the murder and trial and hanging, the latter in 1850. But all was festive two years later, and there was much rice and many ribbons, when Jenny Lind, the Swedish Nightingale, was married at Number 20, with both pomp and music, though Mr. Barnum was not present. At the Pinckney Street end of the Square lived Thomas Bailey Aldrich, in a house that inspired Longfellow to his *The Hanging of the Crane*, and Mr. Aldrich wrote a famous book about a bad boy, though it is not much read today. Celia Thaxter lived a while on the Square, writing poems and some rather good prose, such as *Among the Isles of Shoals*, a sensation in the *Atlantic*. Mr. Howells, who wrote books and edited the *Atlantic*, also lived on the Square.

Not in Mr. Howells' day, but before, there was a time when the Square seethed and boiled with ideas that made the pretty bow windows tremble. In these tall, narrow houses Boston's Abolitionists met to hear Theodore Parker in his best drawing-room style, and often Wendell Phillips.

When the iron was applied to the flesh it gave forth a loud spitting noise, like that of pork a-frying.

They came, too, to meet Jonathan Walker, the slave runner whose right hand carried the brand SS, meaning Slave Stealer, applied by the sovereign court of Pensacola, Florida, where Walker was taken in his nefarious business. Old Whittier came to meet Walker. He looked with smoldering eyes on the seared flesh, then went away to write a famous declamatory poem, "The Branded Hand," long an elocutionary fire bell in Northern

schools. A man who suffered more than Walker did from the
States having split asunder lived on the Square briefly. He was
Edwin Booth, the actor, brother of the great ham, J. Wilkes.
Edwin was a kindly man, no believer in slavery, who was lucky
to escape the lynching that threatened all of his name, after
that dreadful 14th of April in '65. Long after Booth another
person of the theater lived on the Square. She was Minnie Mad-
dern, who married a Fiske, though not the Harvard philosopher.

Around that corner of Mount Vernon Street—just a door or
two from the Square—Francis Parkman lived. He wrote on paper that was marked with string into lines that his hands could
feel—he was all but blind—to compose his books in American
history.

Two doors from Parkman was John Lathrop Motley, minister
to Austria, then to Great Britain, who wrote a notable history of
the United Netherlands. On Mount Vernon, too, abutting the
Square, lived Margaret Deland, whose *John Ward, Preacher*,
shocked almost everybody except the Unitarians.

Even some of the Unitarians were dismayed when lovely
Anne Whitney chipped out of white marble a life-sized statue
of Dame Godiva, complete with horse, and wholly and obviously
both naked and female. Miss Whitney had her home and studio
near the Square after 1872, and here she created her figure of
Samuel Adams, which stands in Washington, and her statue of
Charles Sumner, which sits in Harvard Square in Cambridge;
to say nothing of her fine portrait busts of Mrs. Stowe, Miss L.
Stone and St. Frances Willard. Miss Whitney, despite her Godiva, retained her social and artistic place in Boston, and lived
to be ninety-three. She died in 1915, just when the first taxicabs
were beginning to pollute the air of Beacon Hill.

*Mark Anthony De Wolfe Howe, patriarch of Boston letters,
observed his eightieth birthday [in 1946] yesterday by continu-*

*ing work on his next book. He walked to the Atheneum to con-
sult a few authorities, had lunch at the Tavern Club with his old
colleague, Ira Rich Kent, then returned on foot to his home in
Louisburg Square.*

Mr. Howe lives at Number 16, where he works in his basement library; and every little while, as for half a century past,
another of his charming and authentic volumes on Yankees and
Yankee life appears. A former associate editor of the *Youth's
Companion*, he recalls with a shudder the horrible storm that
blew into the sanctum when, for the first time in a century, a
fictional young man was permitted to kiss a fictional young
woman, in the theretofore chaste and nonbiological columns of
the *Companion*.

Mr. Howe believes that life on Louisburg Square is much
today as it was a hundred years ago. He doesn't mind, much,
when on Christmas Eve thousands of Bostonians swarm over the
bricks of the Square, to peer into the fabulous windows, and
to hear the carolers sing sweetly of mangers and stars and Wise
Men. But I am fairly certain that the Square's first dweller
would not like it any better than he liked the arrival of the Puritans.

Louisburg Square is quite obviously not decaying physically;
nor is there as yet any sign of an intellectual decay. Almost one-
third of the householders are to be found in *Who's Who in
America*, in contrast to a national average of only one in four
thousand. Surely this is no winter of the mind, nor even an Indian summer. The present inhabitants are distinguished in their
several fields, and are writers, publishers, financiers, antiquari-
ans, attorneys, engineers. I doubt that the Square could have
done better at any time in its long and often brilliant life.

Ed Schiefflin struck it rich, and
also left a mystery.

The Man Who Named Tombstone

WHEN the water gets low in the streams
of Douglas County, Oregon, late in summer, twenty, perhaps
fifty old prospectors will converge into the region to look once
again for Ed Schiefflin's lost mine. They have been at it now for
years. Even the war and the man-power situation had little effect on the genuine old-style prospector, the one-mule, one-pick
man, the kind that has been looking for the Schiefflin mine. Some
of them didn't get to hear about the war. They would have been
only mildly interested, anyway, because there is room for but
one idea in the minds of the casehardened old hill rats of the
kind I'm talking about. That subject is a mine, either "lost" or
merely undiscovered, that will prove to be a Golconda.

There are far too many "lost" mines in Oregon and elsewhere
in the West. Most of them are likely figments of imagination in
the minds of men who have lived alone too long. Lone men get
that way. But the Schiefflin affair is founded on something more
solid than the wishful imaginings of hill-goofy prospectors. Ed
Schiefflin was anything but a goof, and there can be little doubt
but that he had struck another rich ledge when he was removed
from the scene. At one time he was the best known mining character in all North America.

Until late in 1877 Ed Schiefflin's life never rose above the
common stream. He was born in Pennsylvania and moved to
Oregon with his parents in one of the covered-wagon trains that

rutted the Oregon Trail across the plains. The gold fever caught Ed early in life. When he was twelve he ran away from home to join the rush into the Salmon River diggings in Idaho. That was in 1862. Salmon River petered out quickly, but young Ed didn't return home. He had caught a disease that few men manage to shake in a lifetime.

For the next fifteen years young Schiefflin ranged all over the West, from coastal Oregon into central Montana. He later told a friend of mine that he had panned eight hundred creeks and rivers during this period, and had driven his pick into more hills than he could remember by name. Most of the time he managed to pan just enough gold to keep him in flour and bacon, but in 1877 the pickings got so poor that Schiefflin did the last possible thing that any hill or desert rat will do; he took a job at wages.

The job was no proletarian one. It was working as a scout in Al Sieber's troop of horsemen who were helping the United States Army to wipe out the Apaches, or at least to hold them within bounds. Under their chief, the able Geronimo, who was soon to require the United States Army to hog-tie him, the Apaches were making life in Arizona rather tough for the pale-faces.

Schiefflin wasn't afraid of any man, red or white, but he just didn't like scouting. Didn't have his heart in it. Always mooning over rocks he picked up. His saddlebags became so filled with this stuff that Chief Scout Sieber had to order Ed to dump it in order to carry food and ammunition. Then Ed would acquire more rocks. One day while on lone patrol in the unlovely hills along the San Pedro River in southeastern Arizona, he saw some rocks that looked particularly good. He got off his horse to inspect them. Yes, sir, they looked like indications of silver.

At this moment Scout Schiefflin had all of $10 due him in wages. He rode directly to Fort Huachuca and told Chief Scout

Sieber what he could do with Ed's job. He drew his $10 and with it bought a second hand pick and a shovel, "borrowed" a little flour and some bacon, and traded his horse for a mule. Then he dug off into the hills alone.

For his headquarters Ed picked the abandoned Brunckow mine, one of the many countless and worthless holes in the ground in that part of Arizona. Herr Brunckow of Germany had begun to dig in this spot in 1858. Not long after he was found with an arrow through his body. Other brave or foolish men had worked at the Brunckow mine, but it never paid out a dollar. Ed paid the mine no heed, using it only as a camp.

Two weeks later Scout Sieber happened along. He found Ed sitting by his campfire. "What you doing, Ed?" he asked.

"Prospecting."

"Where?"

"Over yonder," and Ed waved an arm in the general direction of the San Pedro hills.

"What! Them hills?" exclaimed Sieber. "Geronimo is loose in them hills. You won't find nothing there but your tombstone."

"Take my chances," replied Ed, who wasn't overly talkative. Sieber shook his head and passed on, to tell that Ed Schiefflin was desert-crazy and planning to commit suicide by going into the San Pedro hills.

II

It happened the very next day after Sieber saw Ed—I mean the Big Moment. Schiefflin rose with the sun that morning. Leading his mule he started up a wide draw into the hills. On the way he saw smoke signals from Apache camps. . . . Dot . . . dash . . . dot . . . dash, as some brave warped a blanket to and fro over the fire. They had a Morse of their own. Ed couldn't tell what it meant, but he knew one thing—he'd have to be mighty careful, one man alone, off there in hostile country.

Before long the draw Ed was following divided into two forks. A rabbit scurried up the right fork. Most prospectors play a hunch. Ed took the right fork.

Finally, late that afternoon, Ed saw a spot he thought looked pretty good—a likely piece of ground. He struck his pick into the earth. It might have been so much thick soup, and the pick was buried almost halfway to the handle. Hurriedly pulling back the thin top sod, Ed uncovered a long streak of stuff that nearly blinded him, what with the sun on it and all. It shone like pure silver.

In his pocket Ed had a twenty-five-cent piece, his total capital. He took the coin and placed it on the shiny streak, then pressed. When he withdrew the coin he saw the noble slogan so much revered by all good Americans embossed deeply in the streak of metal. By God, it *was* silver, pure, and soft as putty. Ed Schief-flin sweat mightily and it wasn't from the Arizona sun. Under his feet, he was sure, was a hill, aye, a mountain, of silver. Al Sieber had said all he would find in these hills was his tombstone.

"By Jesus!" said Ed Schiefflin, "I'll call it Tombstone."

Finding silver and getting cash for it are two different things. Ed hacked off a few specimens, but not out of the rock containing the pure metal. He wanted only fair samples of the ledge, and these he took with him to Signal, Arizona, pronto. He had heard that a brother, Al Schiefflin, was working at the McCrack-en mine there.

It was told later that even in the tough town of Signal Ed Schiefflin looked on arrival like the poorest desert rat who ever crawled in off the great open spaces. His clothes were tattered, patched with flour sacks, deer skin, and a piece of horse blanket; his hat was pieced with rabbit skin; his boots were in bad shape; his face was hidden by a curly brown beard. Al Schiefflin, when he came off-shift, did not recognize his own brother in this wild-looking man of rags. But Ed convinced him, and Al took him home. Here Ed produced his silver samples and told Al about the big strike. Al remained very calm. He had heard of plenty of big strikes, that never panned out. "Ed," he said, "I jest ain't interested in rock."

Well, that left Ed with his rock, or silver, or whatever. He would have to get at least a few dollars before he could do anything about his find. Much against his grain he took a pick-and-shovel job in the McCracken mine. He showed his specimens to the foreman. "Jest a good grade of lead," that expert said. It was the same when Ed showed the ore to others. It was pretty discouraging to a man who knew he had a mountain of silver.

Engineer at the McCracken mine was Richard Gird, who had a reputation as a scientific mining man. Ed took his samples into Gird's office. "I'll take a look at them tomorrow," Mr. Gird said. And he did. He also sent a boy to fetch Ed to his office. "I have assayed your ore," he told the prospector. "One piece runs $2,000 to the ton, another $600, and the third only $40. You can't always estimate a claim by two or three samples. Where is your claim?"

Ed had cut his eyeteeth long since. "Over yonder," he said, waving his arms both ways at once. He knew how to answer businessmen.

For the next several days Gird did his best to have Ed tell him where the samples came from. He didn't find out, and at last Gird made a proposition: He would outfit a party of three—himself and the two Schiefflins, if Al cared to go. They would share everything they found three ways. Ed agreed. "There's plenty there for three," he said. The three men struck out of Signal early in February of 1878.

Ed led the party unerringly to the spot he had already named Tombstone Ledge. Gird gave the place a thorough examination and declared that although the pocket was rich, it was also shallow. Several disappointing weeks followed, with Ed doing the prospecting, Gird the assaying, Al the cooking. Then, one day in April, Ed came into camp with that look in his eyes. "Boys," he said, "I've hit the mother lode. She's all jake now."

"Zat so?" remarked Al with sarcasm. "You always was a lucky cuss."

Thus the Lucky Cuss mine got its name. The samples of ore Ed brought in that night assayed $15,000 a ton. This put a wholly new light on matters, and both Al and Gird cheered up and began to sing. As for Ed Schiefflin, it was nothing more than he had expected. A few days later, just to show what a prospector could do when he got up a sweat, Ed uncovered what became the Tough Nut lode, a $75,000,000 strike all by itself. Tombstone, Arizona, was in the making.

III

It was no use trying to be secret about such strikes as the Lucky Cuss and the Tough Nut. Within a few weeks men were trooping into the San Pedro hills by the hundreds, then by the thousands, and fabulous Tombstone came into being promptly. Gamblers, prostitutes, and saloonmen arrived in droves. A newspaper, the Tombstone *Epitaph*, began its celebrated career. The Earps, Curly Bill, John Ringo, John Slaughter, Doc Holliday and the Clantons and the McLowerys were on the way. The hell-roaringest mining town of them all was in the works, and its career outshone Virginia City and Butte in trigger quickness and utter depravity.

The two Schiefflins moved out of Arizona presently and they took $1,000,000 each with them. Gird remained to develop his share of the fortune and to make more millions.

"A million is enough for any man," said Ed Schiefflin.

The Schiefflin brothers parted good friends, and Al went off to live quietly and to die in 1885. Ed announced that as for himself, he had decided to see what all this talk about New York City amounted to. He went up to Denver where he got an outfit of store clothes, including some pretty fine patent leather boots and a silk hat, and then he took a train of steam cars to New York.

Schiefflin made quite a noise in the metropolis. Tombstone was already well-known in Wall Street, and the wild doings of Tombstone's citizens were making other news in the papers. Ed, with his long curly hair and whiskers, and the shiny boots, was sketched by newspaper artists and interviewed. He told the boys that all southeastern Arizona was paved with solid silver. He remarked on the high buildings in New York and sampled champagne at the Waldorf and the Hoffman House. From New York he went to Washington. He was front-page copy here, too, and the same in Chicago. Charity hounds were hot on his trail, begging donations for this or that orphan home, many of which, it turned out later, existed only in name. Ed was a pushover for them all. The old desert rat knew what it was to be hungry. He gave indiscriminately.

But city life didn't fit Ed at all. In 1893, or four years before the world knew that Alaska contained a lot of gold, Ed bought a steamboat and went North, even part way up the Yukon River. But although Ed said he could fairly smell gold up there, his party failed to uncover any of the rich veins that sent the world crazy in 1897–1898.

Returning to San Francisco, Ed sold his steamboat, married a Mrs. Mary E. Brown, and built a mansion on the Alameda. Later he built another big home in Los Angeles. Ed was happy in neither of them. One day in January of 1897 he laid away his silk hat and store clothes and got out his old prospector's rig. Said he was going up to Oregon.

He did go to Oregon, and straight to Douglas County, where he had panned the Umpqua River when he was a lad. He built a cabin and stocked it with provisions. Then he began prospecting along streams that feed the North Umpqua. Men still living say that Ed refused to do any panning or pick work when anyone was around. He was a lone wolf. But his time was running out.

On May 12, 1897, a hunter coming along the lonely trail stopped at Ed's shack with the idea of getting a bite to eat. He found Ed lying face down on the dirt floor of the cabin. It was probably heart disease. There had been no violence. He had been dead several hours. The stove was cold and on it a pot of beans had boiled down to a charred mass.

They took Ed Schiefflin's body to Tombstone and gave him the god-damnedest biggest funeral that town ever witnessed. Bands blared, guns fired, and they buried Ed as he had requested, with his pick and shovel and in his old red shirt. They also built the kind of monument Ed wanted—a small pile of stones such as prospectors use to mark a claim.

I have read Ed Schieffiin's will. He left his real and personal property in Alameda and Santa Clara Counties, California, to his widow, and to her also went $15,000 in bonds of the University of Arizona ("Oughta have a place of book learning," Ed had said.) To his widow and his surviving brother Jay L. Schiefflin, he left an insurance policy of $15,000. The will had been carefully drawn. It continued:

I have no children, but should anyone, at their own expense, prove to the satisfaction of my executors to be a child of mine, to each I give the sum of $50.

The will went on to outline his wish to be buried in Tombstone, and that "none of my friends shall wear crape for me." The will created as much comment in its day as the more recent document of Irvin Cobb.

Today, Tombstone, Arizona, is a sleepy collection of decaying houses and a population of less than eight hundred. The silver has gone—many millions of dollars worth of it—and so has the notorious company of adventurers who followed Ed Schiefflin's trail into the hills. On top of those hills, some three miles west of town, is the pile of rocks that marks Ed's grave.

Eighteen years after Ed Schiefflin's death, a nephew of his, serving with the Canadian forces, was fatally wounded in action near Verdun, France. Before he died he talked a while with a soldier friend and gave him a piece of paper. I know this man and have seen the paper. It is a map, with many written notations, of parts of Douglas County, Oregon. The writing is beyond doubt that of old Ed Schiefflin. Two places on the map are marked "Here." The problem presented by the map is to know certain distances that are outlined. These are in a cypher of Schiefflin's own making and can be learned, apparently, only by experiment—which takes a good deal of time in a region as large and as rough as Douglas County. That is why prospectors have been at work there ever since the map was made known many years ago.

There is one more item. About two weeks before he died, Ed Schiefflin wrote and mailed a letter in which he said: "I have found stuff here in Oregon that will make Tombstone look like salt. [That is, a salted mine and worthless.] This is GOLD."

Douglas County officials and businessmen display complete apathy about Ed's lost mine. However, a dozen or more hard-bitten old hill rats still poke around the creeks of the region, expecting any day to strike the ledge of solid gold that would put them into the Schiefflin class.

$\mathbb{A}$ *notable character of the timber was Okay Fuller,*

King of the Bull Cooks

EARLY in the summer of 1920 I hove into a logging camp in northern British Columbia that was two days by boat from Vancouver. The boat paid little attention to the line's printed schedule and it was late at night when we docked at Deep Bay. As I walked down the gangplank to a log float that was lighted by a dim kerosene lantern, a squat, powerful figure approached me from out of the gloom. It was a man some five feet tall and about as wide across. "You th' new cheater?" he asked. I told him yes, that I was the new timekeeper and scaler.

"That's what I thought," he said. "Foller me." He led the way down a plank walk, past bunkhouses from which came the noise of sleeping loggers, to the camp office. "She's a great layout here," said my guide loudly, "but you gotta be good to last. . . . She's highball."

I was quite sure this fellow was only the bull cook, the camp varlet, and I didn't think a bull cook ought to talk that way to so important a man as a timekeeper and scaler. So I thought I'd put him in his place with some neat sarcasm. "Are *you* the camp push?" I asked. "No," he said, "I ain't the camp push. I'm the bull cook." Then, after a brief pause: "I'm *the* bull cook, the King of Bull Cooks. I'm Okay Fuller."

The voice had the tone of assured authority, and it also carried considerable pride. I looked Okay Fuller over. He was, as I said, about as wide as he was tall. He was somewhere in his late sixties. He had a shaggy beard, grizzled but not yet white, of the General Grant mode, and his face and neck were tanned and wrinkled like an old pair of logger's tin pants. He wore congress shoes, the first I had seen in a long time. His galluses were stupendous, so wide and ruggedly built that they gave the appearance of holding him down into his pants rather than holding them up around him. On the gallus buckles, instead of the usual "Firemen's" it said "Hercules." ("Ordered special from the Hudson's Bay Company," Okay told me.) The top of his pants, I figured, came just below his breastbone.

"Got any drinkin'-likker?" he asked as he lighted a lamp in what was to be my room off the camp office. I told him I hadn't.

"That's no manner of way to come into camp," he said severely. "It usta be that we had men in the woods." I apologized that I had started from Vancouver with a quart but that it had all been used up on the long trip North. "Maybe you'd like a snort, then?" he sort of asked. I said I would.

Okay went back of the office counter and fumbled under it a moment. When he came up he had a small package in his hand.

Without more ado he tore the package from a four-ounce bottle, yanked out the cork, and poured about a third of the contents into a tin dipper of water. The water turned as white as milk. He passed the dipper to me without a word. "What is it," I asked, "jakey?"

"No, it ain't jakey," Okay said. "It's Painkiller. Drink hearty. Good for the bile and eases the kidneys." I drank deep and the stuff hardly hit my stomach before I could feel it in my ankles. I hurriedly gulped down a chaser of water. Okay took the dipper and turned the remaining two-thirds of the Painkiller into it, tossed in a bit of water, and drank it, unflinching. "Painkiller," he announced as though addressing a meeting of the Canadian Medical Association, "is a sovereign remedy against the night chills of the forest. Most especial in the damp an' humid forests of th' Pacific slope."

We talked a while and Okay told me what sort of a camp it was. "This is a mighty fine place," he said, as if he were trying to sell it to me. "You'll like it. Palace in th' woods, that's what I call it. Palace of all th' sultans. Lux'ry such as known only to princes, popes an' po-ten-tates. And me, I'm th' grand eunick. Make yourself to home." Then he went out, slamming the door behind him.

While undressing I looked at the label on the Painkiller bottle. It claimed to be of great thaumaturgic power, good for man and beast, internally and externally, and was graced with a steel engraved portrait of what appeared to be an eminent savant of old-school medicine. I slept very well.

The camp at Deep Bay, I found, was just about average, but Okay Fuller was a bull cook who was anything but average. He liked often to announce that he was king of bull cooks and there is no doubt in my mind that he earned the title, hands down. It should be explained, possibly, that the bull cook of a logging camp doesn't do any cooking. The title is ironic. He feeds the pigs, sweeps out the bunkhouses, cuts and brings in the fuel, washes the lamps, and generally acts as a chore boy around camp. Bull cooks usually are superannuated loggers, and they are often old soaks, bleary of eye and full of loco-motor ataxia, with no spirit. Okay Fuller was none of these.

For one thing there was the way Okay handled his homely duties. He had some two hundred kerosene lamps that must be washed every few days, and filled every other day. Okay called science to his aid. Instead of the long process of wiping the washed chimneys with rag or newspaper, which would have taken hours, he first dipped the chimney into a bucket of clear hot water. After this operation he stood the chimneys on a warm stove. The steam thus generated left the glass as clear as crystal, and the job was done in a moment.

In the matter of splitting large and tough chunks of fir to feed the ravenous box stoves and cookhouse ranges, Okay approached genius. He had the blacksmith pound out a sort of thick metal cartridge with a wedge-shaped end which had a hole in it. He would fill the cartridge chamber with black powder, drive the wedge up to its hilt into the wood block, and touch off a short fuse. The result was a neat quartering of the block. The accompanying noise and smoke, and the smell of powder, pleased Okay immensely. He always said it reminded him of the time he served in the Reil Rebellion in Manitoba and Saskatchewan, Canada's tin-pot "civil war" of the eighties. One time the illusion of battle went further. His own belly well filled with potent Painkiller, he tamped an extra heavy charge into the wedge. The explosion not only blew all hell out of the block, but the gadget burst and part of the metal went through Okay's hat. He had the smithy make a new and larger one. "Make her strong as the Old Rugged Cross," he ordered.

And Okay knew how to deal with bedbugs. They got pretty thick in camp that winter. We tried sprinkling the bed clothes with kerosene, which made our legs raw and sore but didn't seem to have much effect on the pests. One Sunday Okay prodded the engineer into steaming up the locomotive. They rigged up a piece of hose to the condenser, backed the engine up to one bunkhouse after another, and packed them full of steam. It was three or four months before we saw a bug again. In appreciation of this noble work we all chipped in and had a gallon of Demerara rum sent up from Vancouver for Okay, and helped him drink it.

But in spite of his scientific and mechanical interest in things that applied to his own work, Okay Fuller was a hidebound Tory when it came to anything he considered newfangled. Once he evinced a friendly interest when somebody told him a cock-and-bull story about how farmers down in the Fraser River Valley were making fine potable alcohol simply by pouring hard cider into a cream separator and turning the crank; but all other inventions, he said, were leading us to pot.

Although there had never been an automobile or airplane within three hundred miles of camp, Okay was constantly belly-aching about them as works of Satan. The single-shot rifle he had carried in the Reil campaign he held to be a far deadlier and more accurate weapon than the machine gun. He had read something about what he called "the wireless radius [sic] machine" and was sure that no good would come of it. When he spoke of cigarets he fairly frothed.

One day the weekly boat brought a large packing case for the camp. It proved to be a small electric light plant, and with it came an electrician to install the machine and wire the bunkhouses. For days while the work was going forward Okay muttered and seethed. He told how a house owned by his uncle had been struck by lightning the next day after electric lights had been installed. Justifiable act of God, he termed it. His appetite fell off and he took to guzzling more Painkiller and prune juice—which he fermented in his shack—than usual. After he learned how to run the machine I think he rather liked it—that is, privately—as well as the fact that he didn't have to care for two hundred lamps every day or so. But he always claimed that "th' rays of 'lectricity is injurus to th' nekked eye, as well as havin' a bad effec' on the brains."

During that winter a number of small fires occurred in the bunkhouses, caused by newly arrived drunks who went to sleep with lighted cigarets, or by loggers feeding too much "fat" fir into the stoves. And the grading foreman had an unsocial practice of keeping a few cans of dynamite caps under his bunk. Taken all together, the place wasn't so good as an insurance risk. So Paul, the camp foreman, ordered a fire extinguisher for each bunkhouse.

Okay Fuller, of course, was loud in his disapproval of the extinguishers. Every time his eye happened to light on one of the small, bright red objects hanging from a bunkhouse wall, he damned it from the end of its handle to the nozzle. He had, he said, been chief of a volunteer fire department back in Ontario; he was thus an authority and he knew, by God, that no fire extinguisher was so good as water. He went even further, and in a somewhat obscene comparison declared that one healthy poodle dog, male, could lay more fires than all the goddam so-and-so extinguishers put together. "Them red things," he told anyone who would listen, "are trumpery."

It went on this way for months, with Okay harping about the extinguishers. Finally, the foreman got tired of it. "I'll show that old devil what these things will do to a fire," Paul told me one Sunday. He made a pile of packing boxes and excelsior in front of the camp office, and at dinner that noon he invited the entire crew to be present at two o'clock to witness "the magic of Little Pluvius," a phrase he had retained from literature on the subject.

The gang was on hand—Swedes, Finns, Bohunks, and a handful of English-speaking loggers. Paul lighted the pile of rubbish and let it get to blazing good. "Now," he shouted with a flourish of the Little Pluvius, "now you shall see how this small objec' in my hand will relinquish Man's greatest fren' and at the same time Man's greatest enemy."

Paul stepped close to the fire and turned the handle. A small powerful stream of liquid shot forth into the flames. The fire leaped upward all of ten feet. It was so hot Paul had to step back. He shot another round into the fire. It roared louder and higher. Paul's eyes bulged out and there was sweat on his brow. Back of me, in the crowd, I heard Okay Fuller state quite audibly that he had "knowed all along that that Pluto dingus wouldn't put out the fire on the end of a Swede match." He seemed immensely pleased about it.

The fire roared and grew mightily. The audience was moving back a bit. "Get some water," it was Okay's voice I heard. "Get some water," he shouted, "or the whol' jeasley camp'll burn up!" I noted that he already had a pail at his feet. He doused it into the fire, which slackened perceptibly. Okay threw on another pailful and the fire died down to smoke and embers. Okay turned to the audience. "My fren's," he said, and it sounded for all the world like a speech for votes. "My fren's, you can see what that Pluto trumpery amounts to. . . . I thank the good Lord I happened to have a pail of water handy so as to lay low the flames that would have burned us out and made us paupers."

This resounding statement, coupled with the obvious fact that the extinguisher had not put out the fire and the pail of water had, took immediate effect on the crew. Swedes muttered as they tamped a fresh r'ar of snuff into their lips. One of the Hunkies, a small fellow but a most potent orator, made a speech that didn't sound good to Paul, even though he couldn't understand a word. The lone French-Canadian in camp, one Alex Cloutier, said he had heard of a man killed when a fire-extinguisher exploded.

Later, in the privacy of the camp office, Paul and I investigated the liquid left in the extinguisher; it was pure gasoline. Paul charged Okay with doing the job; but there was no proof, and Okay would admit nothing except that God had taken a hand in the matter to show that His water was better than man-concocted chemicals. . . .

The sun was getting to feel warmer. One day I sat on a block in the camp yard where Okay was cutting fuel for the cook-house. The pungent smell of new sawdust told me that the sap was going up the trees. The night before I had heard two cougars snarling and yelling, up on the mountain back of camp—mating cats. Birds were chippering around now. The brook had come to life; I could hear it gurgle over the stones. I remember I thought I would write a poem about it.

Okay had just left the woodyard, wheeling a barrow of fuel into the kitchen. There was a scream, then a wild yell from that direction. I hurried over as fast as I could, but it was all over when I got there. The cookee, or cook's helper, had discovered his wife, who did the dishwashing, in a condition with the boss cook which barristers in Canada describe as adultery. The husband-cookee had thereupon picked up a meat cleaver and started for the couple, shouting that he would cut off his wife's ears and commit mayhem on another part of the cook. Just then Okay happened in with his load of wood. Sensing the situation at once, he picked a hefty stick of fir from his pile and whaled the big cleaver-man over the head, laying him cold and quiet under the sink.

"Hated to do it," Okay told me afterward, "on account adult'ry being something that'll happen with every change of the moon and is mos' likely when the sap's in the wood."

Paul had to fire the entire cookhouse crew. Logging-camp ethics required it. And the incident had an effect on Okay, too. He got very restless. His eyes had a faraway look. Twice he forgot to feed the pigs. And next boat-day he came into the office wearing a rusty old derby hat, a stiff-front white shirt and a rather pretty hook-on tie. "Boy," he said, "I guess I'll go down to Vancouver for a few days. I want to have some work did on my teeth." This, of course, is the standard and classic excuse of the logger who wants to go where he can get things that come in bottles and corsets. I knew Okay Fuller didn't have a tooth in his head, and for the fun of it I told him so.

"Well," he said, with what he meant to be a sensual leer,

"maybe I ain't got no teeth, but one of my gooms is botherin' me."

Okay went down on the boat and I never saw him again. That was long ago. It may be by now that he has gone to the bull cooks' heaven where the lamps are self-fillers, the wood grows exactly the right size to fit a box stove, the bunkhouses are swept each day by perfumed zephyrs, and 110-proof Painkiller oozes out of the trees. Anyway, if Okay Fuller has gone there, I am sure he has the situation well in hand.

*In the old West they called him
the Undertaker's Joy——*

Little Luke Short

ONE of the surest and most respected killers of the old West was Luke Short, a quiet, mild-mannered and colorless little man who looked not unlike that pathetic figure of the cartoons always labeled the Common People. But Luke made a name for himself; in Leadville, in Tombstone and in Fort Worth he was known as the Undertaker's Joy. He never shot but to kill and he killed by drilling a man right between the eyes. Clean job, always.

Luke was born in Arkansas in 1854 and never grew bigger than five feet four inches and 145 pounds. After a bit of riding herd, he opened what he was pleased to call a trading post on the Nebraska-South Dakota border. For a year or so he kept the Sioux thereabout pretty well liquored. But the United States Cavalry swooped down on the post, closed it and put Luke under two guards on a train for jail in Sidney, Nebraska. Luke politely asked to go to the men's room, and never returned; he simply dropped quietly off the moving train and made his way to Leadville.

In hell-whooping Leadville he did very well as a professional gambler. Because he looked so ineffectual—almost pitiful—he found plenty of suckers for his really excellent judgment in respect to the percentages of chance. When a local cardsharp, a blowhard named Brown, took to bullying Little Luke one day at a game of stud, Luke was mildly irritated. "Go 'way, mister,"

Copyright, 1940. by Stewart H. Holbrook. Originally published in *The American Mercury.*

he said, "and don't bother me while I'm workin'. It ain't gen-
teel." Brown became more abusive and finally drew his gun,
thinking to frighten the sad little fellow. Luke shot him as quietly
as possible, between the eyes, before Brown could pull his own
trigger. "The little guy's a fast man," remarked admiring on-
lookers. All Luke said about it was that he hated the sound of
shooting.

When he felt Leadville no longer large enough for his develop-
ing talents, Little Luke moved on to Tombstone, then described
by newspapers and preachers as "the Harlot of the West." He
arrived there in 1881 and set up a faro game. Again the wistful
little man's appeal to suckers was felt and his table was always
crowded. Charley Storms, a local bad man and bully, came in
one night and attempted to break up Luke's game. Bat Masterson, the noted marshal, was present. He took Storms from the
room and warned him to stay outside. But Storms didn't know
when he was lucky. He barged back into Luke's place, waving a
.45 as he entered. Luke didn't trouble to rise from his chair. He
shot Storms very quietly, plumb between the eyes, and was heard
to mutter something about his dislike for loud, unseemly persons in places of amusement. Bat Masterson remarked that he
had never seen such pretty shooting from a sitting position.

Luke never had to draw gun again in Tombstone. Saving a
wad of money, he moved on to Dodge City and in company with
two other men opened a tolerably swell saloon and gambling
hall. Luke had the reputation of being a square gambler, honest
in all his dealings. Moreover, he installed a three-piece band,
then something new. Men and money poured into the place.

Mayor Webster of Dodge City owned a large interest in a rival
saloon and gambling hall and he didn't like the way the boys
were piling into Luke's place. So he passed an ordinance prohibiting music in saloons. Luke quietly complied with the law,

letting his band go. On the next night and from Mayor Webster's saloon, came sounds of a five-piece band. Luke took back his own musical boys and set them to playing. The mayor had Luke arrested, put on a train without trial, and told to keep going.

II

Luke went as far as Kansas City and there planned a coup that resulted in near civil war. He wired his old and good friend Masterson to come to Kansas City. Bat did so. Luke told him sadly that an honest man couldn't operate in Dodge because of a crooked mayor. Bat wired Wyatt Earp, the famous sheriff, who responded at once. Then they collected four other good shooting-men from Caldwell, Kansas, and prepared the assault.

Earp went ahead to Dodge and got a conference with Mayor Webster. "I have several able men coming here in a few days," Earp told his honor, "and we mean to see that Luke Short gets a fair deal here." Faced with Earp, Masterson and their aggregation of gun fighters, the mayor assured the sheriff that no man would be more welcome in Dodge than good old Luke Short. Next day Masterson and Luke, together with their gang, arrived and were met at the station by the mayor's own band and most of the city. It was an ovation.

Luke reopened his place of business and things went smoothly for a time. But the mayor, or at least certain of his cronies, attempted to cramp Luke's style in one way and another. Luke promptly called on the mayor and suggested that he get rid of two deputies Luke didn't like. This was done. Then Luke called on the Dodge sheriff and asked him to fire four of his men. The sheriff did so. Luke next proposed six of his personal friends for the jobs left vacant. This was too much. Mayor and sheriff called on the governor of Kansas for troops "to restore order." They were refused. Luke's pals were appointed to the jobs and Luke himself continued to operate with great success until late in 1884, when he sold out and moved to Fort Worth.

Here he opened the celebrated White Elephant, a combination drinking and gambling establishment, and for more than two years his life was unmarred by unseemly events. Then appeared one Jim Courtright, an ex-convict turned racketeer who was hired by higher-ups of Fort Worth to collect protection money from saloons and gambling dens. Luke, genial soul, paid protection up to a certain point. When Courtright tried to raise the ante, Luke refused. "That sum is too much for a square joint to pay," he said, "and I'm not goin' to pay it."

That evening, which happened to be February 8, 1887, Luke and Courtright met on the street in front of the White Elephant. Courtright reached for his gun. Before he could get it from its holster Luke had shot him once, between the eyes. "That feller ain't got no sense of proportion," Luke said sadly, and with apparent regret, as he returned his smoking gun to his pocket. When he heard of the affair, Wyatt Earp remarked that some day, perhaps, would-be tough guys would learn to leave Little Luke alone.

Luke was tried for murder and acquitted. He followed his occupation of gambler until September 8, 1893, when he died peacefully at Queda Springs, Kansas, of disease, as befitted a quiet man of sedentary habits. A bullet had never even parted his hair.

G il Patten wrote 208 books, mostly about

Frank Merriwell

THERE died in San Diego, California, one day not long ago, a tall, white-maned old gentleman listed in the telephone directory as Gilbert Patten. He was almost eighty, and he had long outlived his day, for to millions of middle-aged Americans he was Burt L. Standish, creator of the peerless Frank Merriwell, and Frank had died a long time before. I can think of no other fictional characters so real to my generation as those who peopled the Merriwell saga.

Today's sons and grandsons have never heard of the Merriwell boys, for they are deader even than the Alger heroes, and several attempts at resuscitation proved dismally futile. Yet the Merriwell story called for 208 books, and their total printings, as nearly as can be ascertained, ran to 125,000,000 copies. That would put them up, or down, into the Horatio Alger class. Their heyday came near the end of the Alger period. For eighteen years first Frank, then his younger brother Dick, lived, breathed, and won games for Yale College, and spurned the unspeakable Harvard cads as they did alcohol, cigarets, and coffee. I am a little surprised that the great university in New Haven never saw fit to grant an honorary degree to the non-Eli who gave Yale more favorable publicity than did any of its graduates.

Although I never got to Yale, my heart was set on going there and my reason was not William Graham Sumner, nor Billy Phelps, nor even Ted Coy. It was because Frank Merriwell had

been a student there. I knew, of course, that the Merriwell stories
were fiction and that fiction was somehow or other not really
true, yet I could not get out of my mind that somewhere there
simply must be a genuine Frank Merriwell, complete with keen
gray eyes, strong chin, muscles of steel, and a heart of gold.
And fearless too.

"You are a cheap cad," Frank told the big overdressed bully.
That bully was a Harvard cad, too. Almost any volume of the
Merriwell series was a libel on Harvard and all it contained.

Frank Merriwell first appeared in 1896, in *Tip Top Weekly*,
a five-cent "dime novel" established specifically for the Merriwell saga by the venerable firm of Street & Smith, New York. In
that first story Frank was a student at a fictitious preparatory
school named Fardale Academy. He seemed, then as later, to be
often suffering from sprained ankles, broken hands, and one
thing and another, but he was always ready with the three-base
hit in the ninth inning, no matter how dreadful the injury. Going
on to Yale in due course, he naturally became the finest athlete
there, and there, in addition to more sprained ankles, he had to
contend with the crooked men of Harvard, and to lesser degree
the crooked men of Brown, Amherst, Dartmouth, and other low-
life and gangster-ridden colleges, all of whom were bent on getting Frank drunk, or drugged, or kidnapped just before the Big
Game, either football or baseball. Or, they might simply try to
bribe him to throw the contest. It was all the same in the end,
and the end was a glorious Yale victory over the slimy imps of
Cambridge or wherever, and against practically insuperable
odds.

When by the very nature of college, Frank at last had to leave
Yale—taking all of the scholastic honors at graduation—Dick
Merriwell was about to enter good old Fardale Academy. Dick
followed more or less in his brother's footsteps, although he was
never quite so popular, even though he pitched with either hand

and the bewildered batters never knew which way the ball would curve; whereas Frank, a straight righthander, had to get along as best he could with a double curve and a ball that merely leaped a foot above its natural trajectory just as the batter took swing. Incidentally, more than one youth of my generation like to have thrown his arm from its socket in attempts to get a baseball to jump like a startled rabbit in the Frank Merriwell manner.

Both Merriwells, you may be certain, performed as fullbacks on the gridiron. They stroked the varsity crews. In field and track, either of the Merriwell boys commonly entered in the 100-yard dash, the quarter mile, the mile, pole vault, the broad and high jumps, and the weight throwing. If at the last minute some slicker added a discus throw to the program, thinking thus to beat a Merriwell in one event, Frank picked up the big plate, cuddled it a moment in his arm, then tossed it to hell and gone.

No, sir, there was just no stopping the Merriwell boys. When both had finally emerged from college, they went around the world with a baseball team, doing a little big-game hunting on the side, being captured by savages, and having other adventures. Accompanying them, in school and out, were a set of characters whose names are sure to light up the eye of graying Americans today. Harry Rattleton (he stuttered), Ephraim Gallup (Vermont farm boy), Barney Mulloy (with full Hibernian accent), Bart Hodge, Bruce Browning—these were as real to us as Frank himself. Nor was Frank wholly without biological urge. One week it was dark Inza Burrage, again it was blonde Elsie Bellwood. (Frank went so far as to "embrace" them.) Looking back on these love affairs, it would seem that Frank played the two girls against each other for the best part of eighteen years. At last they married. I forget Dick's girl, but Frank married the handsome Inza, at about the time World War I got under way.

Interest in the Merriwell boys petered out with tragic swiftness. By the end of the war they had been forgotten.

The Merriwells' creator was born Gilbert Patten in 1866, in Corinna, Maine. His father wanted him to be a carpenter and thus earn the stupendous wage of $2.50 a day. Young Gil wanted to write, and he was barely seventeen when he sold his first short story, "A Bad Man," to Beadle & Adams of New York for $6. He never wrote another short story. His next effort was a short novel, for which he received a check for $75. His next was a bit longer and brought $150, and he became a regular contributor to the Beadle & Adams tripe factory.

For the next twelve years he ground out a 20,000-word novel a week for the house, chiefly Westerns. He moved to New York for a while, and made a trip through the Far West. In 1895 he returned to Maine and settled down in Camden. Here in that year he received a long letter from O. G. Smith, president of Street & Smith, just then engaged in taking the dime-novel field away from Beadle, asking him to consider a new series built around an American youth attending a preparatory school, who should finally go to college. The basic idea was a type of story which should inspire American youth to high ideals in the field of sport and life generally.

Patten told me, in his old age, that the moment he got the letter from Smith he knew that this was to be his field. He had long since tired of the absurdities of the Western story and was ready for absurdities in some other line. He wrote Smith, agreeing to turn out a 20,000-word story a week for $50. *Frank Merriwell; or, First Days at Fardale* was the first story. It must have been the answer to Mr. Smith's prayer for something to print. For the next decade and a half S & S printed *Tip Tops* by the million; and every little while they reset the Merriwell stories in smaller format and put two of them together to make a volume in the Medal Library, price ten cents.

Tip Top Weekly was grouped, in the ignorant minds of preachers and school teachers of the time, with the other so-called dime novels, like *Nick Carter Weekly*, *Jesse James Weekly*, *Young Wild West*, and *Buffalo Bill*. This was not fair, for *Tip Top* stood alone. It also stood for all manly attributes, less alcohol, tobacco, and unorthodox amour, which were banned not because they were immoral of themselves, but because they prevented an athlete from doing his best.

"I do not use liquor," Frank's voice remained on an even keel, "and I will thank you to put away that flask. Don't you know that you can't drink *that* and play good baseball?"

Tip Top should have been excepted from the general run of dime novels. No boys ran away from home, or tried to hold up a passenger train from anything suggested in the Merriwell series. And in time most parents came to recognize the divergence, and *Tip Top* was brought into the parlor from the haymow. Patten told me he had received at least 50,000 letters, many from parents, commenting on the fine qualities of the Merriwell boys.

When the Merriwells finally were done, Patten tried to follow with a Cliff Sterling. Cliff got the brush-off; the kids wouldn't have him. Nor would they accept a Rex Kingdon. So, Patten edited a pulp magazine successfully for a few years. He wrote a play much used by amateurs. He tried again to hit the juvenile fancy by dredging up a Frank Merriwell Junior. But the old magic had gone. It had gone, too, when the movies made a Merriwell series; and when radio tried out the former great Yale athlete. Then, in 1941, Patten brought out a full-length book, *Mr. Frank Merriwell*, in which the original Frank was brought down to date as a middle-aged citizen. Few people bought or read it.

When I knew him, Mr. Patten was in his early seventies. Tall and tanned, of rugged build, his great leonine head would have made a superb model for the head of a Mountain Man, or a Pioneer. He seemed always to be in good humor, and if he ever complained because a new generation would not accept his wares, I never heard him. His sense of humor was immense; and, with a Maine accent untouched by forty years of living in all parts of the United States, he could tell Down East stories that had the full, genuine flavor.

The last time I saw him, I asked the old gentleman why his later stories did not catch on. He knew the answer. "It was," he said, "because I was too old to know what sort of youth the present younger generation admires and looks up to. I tried to find out, but never did. And I don't know yet."

War Horse Boose still sells *I.W.W.* papers and songbooks.

The Last of the Wobblies

THE gloom of late winter afternoon draped and permeated all Portland. Wind whipped the harbor wildly. It flapped awnings of the joints along Burnside Street. Rain streaked the windows and glistened like rhinestones as the lights began to come on, one by one, in Erickson's, in the Valhalla, in a hundred other places known the world over to men who work outdoors with their hands. Dusk was coming down on Burnside, the most celebrated skidroad in Oregon, or on earth.

At the corner of Third stood a figure familiar to this spot on Saturdays for two decades and more. Arthur Boose, the Wobbly paper boy, in fact the last of the Wobbly paper boys, here or elsewhere, a bundle of the *Industrial Worker* under one arm, the other supporting the husky overcoated man with a stout cane. . . . Get your copy of the *Worker*, he was saying, get your double dose of industrial unionism hot off the griddle, learn the truth about the labor fakers, get into the One Big Union, be a man, five cents buys a complete education for any scissorbill, get your *Worker* now. . . . High wind, low rain, sunshine, sleet, or snow, or even troublesome cops, they are all the same to Arthur Boose, the Old War Horse, and the Saturdays of twenty-odd years have found him on the Skidroad in Portland doing his level damnedest to convert the dehorns, the scissorbills, the finks, the Mister Blocks, the Hoosiers, homeguards, hoboes and bums into Rebels; and the only Rebels who count with Boose are members of the Industrial Workers of the World—the Wobblies.

It is perhaps necessary, for those who came in late, to explain that the I.W.W. commonly called Wobblies are likely the most distinctive and certainly the most American labor group the United States has ever known. Founded in 1905, militant, aggressive from the start, and as swiftly mobile as their membership which is (or was) composed of itinerant workers, the Wobblies raised more plain and particular hell in their twenty years of operations than any other union before or since. They organized the working stiffs of the woods, the mines, the harvest fields, the construction jobs, and occasionally the textile and the steel slaves. They staged strikes or riots in Lawrence, Massachusetts; in McKee's Rocks, Pennsylvania; in Calumet, Michigan; Virginia, Minnesota; Wheatland, California; Everett, Washington; and many another place. Wherever the Wobblies were, there too was battle.

The Wobblies were out for nothing short of Revolution, immediate, manifest, and complete, and to this end they bent their every energy. No voting for them, no peaceful revolution. They were lighting the fire for the Red Dawn which many of them devoutly believed would blaze up from behind the mountain at the very same moment the money palaces of Morgan and Rockefeller exploded and turned into rubble, the result of well-placed charges of 90 per cent stumping powder. World War I conditions took heavy toll of the Wobs, though they rallied and flared again in 1919 and appeared to be going pretty strong until internecine warfare ripped them into two factions. By 1925 their ranks had dreadfully thinned. Nor did the depression revive them. Their aging leaders joined the Communists, the Socialist Labor Party, Technocracy, and most of their rank and file went into the C.I.O., or even into the A.F. of L. But not Old War Horse Boose.

II

Mellowed today, yet truculent enough in matters pertaining both to Capital and "the right kind of Unionism," Arthur Boose lives a spartan life and keeps bachelor quarters in a corner room of the Chester Rooms ("Reasonable Rates"), a venerable building along the Portland waterfront. He is a man of medium height, broad-shouldered, with a fine head topped by a heavy growth of silver hair. Always clean-shaven, except for a neatly trimmed mustache, he might make you think of a banker—God save us—were it not for the man's eyes. In them smolders the light that comes not from bonds and mortgages, nor yet from Arcturus, but from some inner fire, kindled perhaps from the same coals that burned in the eyes of old Johann Most, the anarchist of demoniac intensity from whom the young Arthur Boose of long years ago learned that things were not as they should be, that peace on earth and good will to men were a delusion so long as the System prevailed.

Boose is always dressed in quiet good clothes of heavy blue serge, and wears a spanking old-fashioned watch chain across his vest. He has carried a cane since that time, early this century, when a big white pine log came whirling down a Wisconsin rollway and crushed his leg. He was born in 1878 in Milwaukee of German immigrant parents, and in his speech is yet a faint trace of accent in respect to "w" and "v."

Arthur Boose's mother died when he was six. Ten years later he quit school and home, to work in logging camps as a cantdog man, then as a teamster, in the pineries along the Chippewa and other streams. It was near Phillips where his leg was crushed, and while convalescing in Milwaukee he attended art school. Painting today is his only hobby. While recovering from his injury, too, young Boose attended lectures in the Milwaukee Freethinkers' Hall, a place of hellish reputation among the godly, and there one evening he listened spellbound while the aging Johann Most, wild-eyed and wild-whiskered, the very model for the cartoonists' Anarchist, told of the need for revolution by the working class; and Lucy Parsons, widow of the Haymarket Martyr, related the manner by which the rulers of creation kept the working class in their places.

"Those two lectures made a great impression on me," Boose recalls. "I talked with Mrs. Parsons afterward. She was a brilliant and altogether wonderful woman. I came away convinced that the world could be bettered, even though I myself wasn't quite ready to do anything about it."

For the next few years Boose followed, as they say, the wheat harvests, and worked in logging camps. He drove teams on construction jobs. And in 1909, in Minneapolis, he took out the Little Red Card that made him a Wobbly. Since that day he has never been in arrears with I.W.W. dues, nor has he ever joined another union. If there is merit in consistency, then Wobbly Boose is a man of merit. Through good times and bad—very bad—through days and weeks and months and years in jails, workhouses, penitentiaries, through days of danger and riot, under his real and his phony names, Old War Horse Boose has never wavered. The Wobblies are *right*, and their aging stalwart would rather be right than popular.

III

Wobbly Boose came first into national prominence in 1916. The First World War was under way and two years old. Wages in most industries had been going up, and the iron miners of the great Mesabi range in Minnesota wanted more pay. They started a half-hearted and wholly unorganized strike. Boose was in charge of the I.W.W. hall at Duluth. Quickly seeing that their strike wasn't getting anywhere, a group of Finn miners sent a telegram to the Finnish newspaper in Duluth asking for an organizer, and Boose was asked if he would go. Turning over the Wobbly hall to another, Boose went to Aurora, a Mesabi mine town, and staged a couple of hot meetings. Local police, naturally dominated by the mining companies, put Boose in jail on a charge of "inciting to riot."

The War Horse was now stabled, but there was kick in him yet. Talking through the bars of the tiny jail in Aurora, he urged the miners to spread news of the burgeoning strike to all parts of the range as rapidly as possible. Spread it like forest fire, he said. That night a young Finn, Ormi something-or-other, started the spreading. He had no horse, no train of cars, so out of Aurora that evening he walked until he was beyond the vision of mine police. Then he ran.

In the prime of young manhood, the Finn ran swiftly through the twilight, traveling like a shadow blown by a soft Mesabi wind. At Biwabik he roused the boys, then on to McKinley, and so on to Virginia, where he waked the secretary of the Finnish Brotherhood Lodge. Next morning few miners showed up for work anywhere along the eastern section of the range.

At the time of his arrest, Boose also managed to get word of events to I.W.W. headquarters in Chicago, and now to the range came a whole pack of able organizers, among them Sam Scarlett, Elizabeth Gurley Flynn, Frank Little, later lynched at Butte, and Carlo Tresca, whose murder at Fifth Avenue and Fifteenth Street in 1943 still mystifies Manhattan police. At almost the same time that the organizers arrived, shooting started in the mine towns. Several miners were killed, and so were a couple of mine police.

Boose was moved from Aurora and confined in the jail at Virginia, then bailed out by a saloonkeeper. He promptly mounted the platform in the Finn hall and addressed a mass meeting of strikers. He said, among other things, that although the I.W.W. did not believe in the use of violence, nevertheless workingmen

must protect themselves; and now that the "mine Cossacks" had
begun killing "innocent workers," it was perhaps time for the
workers to arm themselves. He went on to speak of rats and parasites, and wound up by saying: "Parasites should be extermi-
nated!"

"Fine, fine!" shouted Carlo Tresca, chairman of the meeting.

"For every miner killed," Boose went on, "a mine cop must
die!"

This kind of talk was a great mistake, Boose says today.
Eugene Debs had made the same kind of mistake in an earlier
day, and so had Bill Haywood.

Well, the clubbing and shooting continued, and also the arrests of Wobbly organizers and sympathizers. The strike com-
mittee, figuring Boose was now a man marked for the cops, sent
him to Duluth, just as newspapers came out with word of an indictment for murder against him and four other Wobblies. Boose,
who seldom bothered to read capitalist newspapers, knew nothing
of the indictment. A friendly attorney in Duluth told him about
it and advised him to get out of there. Boose hid until train-time,
while cops hunted him, then went to Minneapolis. It was still too
warm. Wobbly Frank Little showed up with a copy of the newspaper in which Boose was quoted as saying that all of the mine
cops ought to be killed. It also played up the murder indictment
in a front-page box.

Now began a time of great danger for Boose. He knew he had
nothing to do with the murder for which he had been indicted;
it had occurred before he delivered his fiery speech in Virginia.
But Little and Haywood warned him that would make no dif-
ference; he was a Wobbly organizer, hence he would be rail-
roaded. They urged him to leave Minnesota. Boose went to Wisconsin to work a while in the woods, then to Chicago. Here he
met Haywood, Gurley (The) Flynn, Joe Ettor and other Wob
leaders, and they all told him he was "hot," to get going to far

places and to stay until the Mesabi strike was done. Changing his
name to Arthur Fritz, Boose grabbed a fast freight and landed in
Oklahoma, where he went to work driving team on a railroad
construction job. Early in 1917 Haywood detailed him to go into
the western oil fields to organize the working stiffs. He did, then
was called to Tulsa to take charge of the I.W.W. hall. He now
dropped "Fritz" and became Boose again.

On September 5, 1917, the so-called Palmer Raids took place
all over the country. Radicals and persons suspected of independent thought were arrested and jailed all the way from Maine
to California. Oddly enough, the raiders overlooked Arthur
Boose, secretary of the I.W.W. at Tulsa. But not for long. On the
28th, three large, rather grim men attended one of Boose's edu-
cational talks in the Wobbly hall, then arrested and took him to
jail. "I was charged," he remembers, "not only with being a
fugitive from the murder charge in Minnesota, but with almost
every crime I had ever heard of, including lack of what is commonly called patriotism."

They took Boose to Chicago and there, throughout much of
1918, he and 165 other Wobblies and sympathizers were tried
on five counts charging conspiracy to obstruct the war. The evidence, including tons of Wobbly papers, pamphlets and even correspondence, much of it illegally seized, would have filled three
freight cars. The correspondence was particularly damning.
"Haywood was always careless of his mail," says Boose, who
adds that it was matter from Haywood's correspondence, all of
which tactically should have been destroyed as soon as read, that
was used as evidence to convict Boose and several of the other
defendants.

Ninety-three of the Wobblies were found guilty in various
degrees and were sentenced to from one to twenty years in prison.
(Haywood, out on bail, skipped to Russia, where he died.) Boose

drew five years, and was released on expiration of his time in June of 1922.

While in prison at Leavenworth, Boose read constantly in such works of philosophy and economics as he could lay hands on. They merely confirmed his beliefs that the Wobblies had the right idea, or at least the best idea that had so far been put forward, for a new and a better world; and when he came out of the Big House, he picked up where he had left off. The stiffs must be educated and organized. Incidentally, of his jail and prison days, Boose recalls that the Christmas of 1917, spent in what he calls the Cook County Can in Chicago, was brightened considerably by receipt of gifts of a necktie, two pairs of socks, and a handkerchief, from Helen Keller. Each of the ninety-three prisoners received like presents from the famous blind woman.

IV

In the autumn of 1922, War Horse Boose, by then one of the most celebrated of Wobblies, started west on a speaking tour which eventually took him to Portland, Oregon. He soapboxed during the longshore and all of the lumber strikes of the 1920's and 1930's. Arrests on what appear to have been trumped-up charges were a regular thing. Once, in Walla Walla, Washington, Boose had barely hit town and had not yet had time to set up his flag and soapbox when a motorcycle cop arrived and took him to jail. "Quickest pinch I ever knew," he says today. There were many other pinches, too, one on the charge of "profanity" ("I said that the Bible shouters sell Jesus Christ over the counter like so much sugar"); another on a charge of "obstructing traffic," something Boose was always careful not to do. Incidentally, he has been arrested, on one charge or another, and always in connection with his work, in Aurora, Virginia, and Minneapolis, Minnesota; in Tulsa and Drumright, Oklahoma; in Great Falls,

Montana; and in Portland and Walla Walla. Cops have slugged
him. So have patriots. Judges have lectured and fined him. His
meetings have been broken up with fire, with water, with stink-
balls, eggs, brickbats, with shouting and rioting.

Yet Old War Horse Boose, a name applied by admiring Wobblies many years ago, is still packing the rigging, as they say
of active I.W.W. organizers, and he remains a cheerful and
wholly unreconstructed Wobbly. "I'd prefer anarchism," he told
me one day recently, "for that is the highest and finest form of
civilization possible. But we aren't ready for it yet. We aren't
even ready for the kind of world the I.W.W. wants. It takes
time." He considers Communists both comical and hopelessly
entangled in dogma. He would as soon think of voting the Re-
publican as the Communist ticket.

It irritates the War Horse to call him the Last Wobbly. He
claims there are some twenty thousand members of the I.W.W. in
this country and Canada. Maybe there are, but they are not in
evidence in the Pacific Northwest, the real home of the Wobs;
but Arthur Boose is. Everyone familiar with Portland's Skidroad
district knows him as the only Wobbly paper boy left in the
Northwest, and as nearly as I can learn, the only one on earth.
He peddles his papers, as related, every Saturday, no matter
the times nor the weather, and along with the *Worker* he sells
a few copies of I.W.W. pamphlets, and the latest edition (the
twenty-eighth) of the justly famous Little Red Song Book, which
contains a good picture of the late Katie Phar, songbird of the
Wobblies, who rallied the boys with her sweet voice from 1910
to her death in 1943. The twenty-eighth edition of the song book,
like all the others since it was composed, contains Joe Hill's Last
Will, "written in his death cell on the eve of his judicial murder
by the authorities of the State of Utah, Nov. 18, 1915."

Old-time Wobs, passing through Portland, usually call on
Boose, who is the official, stationary delegate of the I.W.W. in

that city. They often find him brewing a cup of coffee on the gas plate in his room, his table covered with brushes and water colors, at work on some forest scene, his favorite motif. For an old-time Wobbly, Boose will put away his colors and brushes, and talk of the great days when the Wobbly brand of revolution ran like fire through the wheat, the mines, the woods of the West; when the West fairly reeked of Wobblies, and Wob organizers hung stiffly from bridges and trestles by their necks, or died on the bloody decks of the *Verona* in Everett Harbor, or went down in the choking dust of Wheatland or Bisbee. . . . Aye, my lads, those were great days, days when working stiffs had nothing to lose but their chains, unless on occasion their lives. Almost alone, the Old War Horse has survived them, unchanged.

The moment he died he went into American legend——

Kit Carson

WHEN John C. Frémont, the Great Pathfinder of American history, was preparing for his first expedition in 1842, he looked around for a likely guide. One Kit Carson of whom he had never heard applied for a job. Frémont asked him if he had had any experience as a Rocky Mountain guide. Kit then made his classic reply. "Reckon so," he said as he spat a full twenty feet. "A ten-prong buck warn't done sucking when I last sit on a chair."

It was true. No man, not even Dan'l Boone, was on the move so continuously as Kit Carson. As early as 1830 the Rockies, the Columbia River and the Pacific shore were old stuff to him. His ability to go anywhere without a compass and to come out where he had planned was said never to have been equaled. The record would indicate that he was the greatest Pathfinder of them all, but he had no object in his roving other than to allay his restlessness. Otherwise, he would loom much larger in sober American history, instead of being relegated to folklore and frontier literature.

A small man physically, he was five feet six inches and never weighed more than 160 pounds, all of which was steel spring. The man was almost indestructible. He was perhaps the softest-spoken and most modest of all the boys who took on grizzly bears hand-to-hand, fought Comanches to a standstill and could exist for days merely by chewing his buckskin leggings.

Copyright, 1940, by Stewart H. Holbrook. Originally published in *The American Mercury.*

Kit was born in Kentucky in 1809 and moved to Missouri with his family. Apprenticed to a saddler, he immediately ran away and was soon acting as hunter and guard for a wagon train trading into Mexico. He got his first hostile Indian when he was sixteen by drilling him through the head at 75 yards. He went out with several trapping expeditions for the Rocky Mountain Fur Company, always returning to Taos, which he liked to call his home even if he was seldom there.

The first trip with Frémont wasn't very exciting, but there was plenty doing on the others. At Klamath Lake in the Oregon country, the Frémont party was surrounded by hostile Modocs. Kit crawled on his belly out onto the vast lava beds, alone, and picked off a Modoc here and there until the red men thought they were trying to fight a devil, and went away. Kit led his party into California. Here a band of thirty redskins ran off with a number of horses belonging to the party. With a man named Godey, Kit followed the thieves, finding them encamped in the Sierras. Kit and Godey proceeded to attack the thirty Indians and routed them, killing four and taking the scalps for proof. They also retrieved the horses.

Then the Mexican war broke out. Apparently without orders, Kit marched alone one night on the Spanish fort at the Golden Gate. He had a mess of common rat-tail files in his pocket. With sentries all around him, Kit spiked every gun in the fort and returned to his own camp before daylight. "I reckon," he said, "they won't fire them guns now." It was one of his greatest exploits.

Frémont was often in trouble and was finally cut off from other American troops by a superior force of Mexicans. Taking a Lieutenant Beale with him—"Got to make it legal," he said— Kit crept through the Mexican lines and got word to Commodore Stockton, who sent relief to the Americans. Kit was mentioned in orders again. Stockton converted Frémont's men into a navy battalion of mounted riflemen, and Kit went along. The force sailed for San Diego and Kit put in the worst week of his life, being horribly seasick. He never forgot this voyage and often swore that he would sail no more "so long as mules has got backs."

II

By this time the imperial Americans had proclaimed California to be a territory of the United States, and Kit performed the feat that made him a national character. Frémont made him a lieutenant, gave him fifteen picked men, and sent him overland to Washington with dispatches reporting California's capitulation. On September 15, 1846, Kit and his crew rode out of Los Angeles on the 3,000-mile trip, much of it through hostile country. Two days out they ran into a large village of Apaches. Kit rode ahead alone, into the village. He spoke to the red men in their own tongue to such a good effect that he and his men were allowed to pass. But a white villain barred the way. He was General Stephen W. Kearny, heading west with an army to subdue California. Word that it was already in American hands did not please him. He forbade Kit to continue to Washington. Kit obeyed but warned the General that the way west was full of danger just then. Unheeding, Kearny ordered the march. Fifty miles from San Diego they ran into an ambush. Kit had a horse shot from under him, Kearny himself was twice wounded, and forty Americans were killed.

But the army got through, and now, with both Kearny and Frémont on the glory ground, Kit was permitted to start for Washington again. This time he made it with great speed and delivered the dispatches that electrified the nation. It was the Lindbergh feat of the day, and Kit Carson's became the front-page name. But the Government didn't treat the hero very well. His army commission had never been confirmed and he found he had no pay coming for having risked his life continuously and also for having performed a feat that few Americans could have accomplished. Fed up with army and political knavery, he turned to ranching. It was altogether too quiet. He up and bought more than a thousand sheep in New Mexico and drove them through bad-Indian country to settlements on the Eastern edge of the Rockies, where he sold the lot. It appears to have been his only business venture. He now hiked over the Rockies to San Francisco, and was feted as a hero in that wild city. He turned to guiding bodies of American troops against marauding Mexicans and Indians, and once led ten men on an attack that routed between three hundred and four hundred Indians.

When the shot was fired at Sumter, Kit didn't know where he stood. This war over slavery was something entirely beyond his simple comprehension. But Frémont, now a major general, knew a good man when he saw one. He personally lined Kit up for the North and saw that he was made a brevet brigadier general of volunteers. It was a notable appointment. During the next seven years Kit led his troops against Indians who saw the Civil War as a time to exterminate the palefaces. He held them in check, often cracking down on them hard, and fought some of the fiercest guerrilla warfare this country has seen. They managed to get General Carson into gold braid for a few days, but he presently turned up in his old buckskin togs and wore them until the end. All the fighting was just good fun to him, compared with learning to write his name, which he thought rather foolish but finally accomplished. A number of historians have said in print that Carson's work on the frontier during the Civil War was one of the most necessary campaigns of the time, and brilliantly conducted.

He continued his efforts at subduing the wild lands until 1867. Then, tired and broken by more hardships than most men live through, he resigned. The last of his three wives was dead. Kit went to Fort Lyon and the soldiers there were happy to give the old hero what he asked for. It wasn't much: a bed of buffalo robes on the floor of a house in Officers' Row. He made his will and asked to be buried in Taos. He was really ill. The post doctor forbade him his pipe and put him on a diet. Kit grumbled no end about a man not having his pipe, and on May 23, 1868, he could stand it no longer. He lay on his buffalo robes and said: "Bring me some fust-rate doin's. Bring me a buffalo steak, a bowl of coffee, and my pipe." The Army doctor warned Kit that such a meal would kill him. "Don't matter," said Kit. He ate two pounds of steak, drank a quart of coffee and smoked his pipe. He allowed he felt a heap better, and then he turned over and died very quietly. He had a funeral with full military honors, and his body was taken to Taos.

Men who knew him only by reputation were astonished that such a daring man should have died with his boots off. Those who had ranged and soldiered with him were not. They said Kit was too tough to be killed; he simply had to wear out. And that's what he did, aged almost fifty-nine, and wrapped in buffalo robes; and he went directly into more American legends and dime novels than any man except Jesse James and Dan'l Boone, who had been Kit's grandfather.

Macloy didn't know what the war was about, but it was all right.

The Greatest Corporal Since Napoleon

THE moment he jumped down off the troop train and yelled ". . . the Kaiser" at the top of his lungs, I knew that this drafted rookie from the Maine woods was something out of the ordinary. All the others seemed awed at the braid and gold bars of officious shavetails and the barking of us sergeants. Not so Mac.

He gave his name as Henry Macloy and said he came from Bangor, Skowhegan, Calais, Moosehead Lake "and all them places." He had registered for the 1917 draft at Skowhegan.

Mac was of medium height, short of leg, and was possessed of the damnedest pair of shoulders seen since Man came down out of the trees to live. They were vast. He was dressed, that day he arrived at Camp Devens, Massachusetts, in what loggers of the time considered nobby clothes—the coat came nearly down to the knees and the pants were of the best 1906 peg-top style. Their color was that sickish purple-blue, a shade ordinarily preferred by drunk lumberjacks when buying a new suit in town.

One side of Mac's coat was wrinkled like that of a Merino sheep, caused, so Mac carefully explained, by his sleeping against a radiator in a Bangor hotel the night before. His breath was aromatic, so we frisked him hopefully. There was nothing. "Took last snort on th' train," he said, and added that he sure was sorry he didn't have a drink left "for you gen'rals."

I liked the way Mac handled his feet. He had gone down-river on a score of white-water streams—a true river driver—and he was quick and light as a mink. He readily learned the School of the Soldier, Dismounted, and he handled his Springfield beautifully. He never smoked and often said loudly that a man who used them damned cig'rets wouldn't stop at nothing. But he chewed huge quantities of Black B-L Plug and spat copiously at drill, guard mount and retreat. He held that the chewing of tobacco was a positive preventive against consumption, of which he was in as much danger as a bull moose in Aroostook County, Maine, and he never did learn that there was a regulation against chewing in ranks. On occasion he could be a notable non-spitter, holding the juice for an hour at a time. When he did spit, it was something to see, and to hear.

I figured Mac was already a pretty darned good soldier and recommended to the captain that he be made a corporal. This was done. Mac was happy at the $6 added pay. He also pretended to take his two chevrons seriously, although he really scorned the Army and all soldiers of any army, anywhere. I liked to hear him give ironical and long-winded talks to his squad about how General Grant—sometimes it was General Washington—had said that corporals were the backbone of the army.

Mac liked the women, any woman, and I have every reason to believe he was successful with them. None of the slogans of 1917, such as "Five Minutes with Venus may mean Five Years with Mercury," caused him so much as to shift his chew. I recall marching our battery, in compliance with an august General Order from the War Department, to a cantonment theater to witness the showing of a hygienic moving picture entitled *Fit to Fight*. This film depicted the physical evils, even horrors, that follow sexual immorality, especially those that follow the sexual immorality of enlisted soldiers. Every one who was in O.D. in 1917 will remember it. The latter part of the film was gruesome enough, consisting of close-ups of some horrible examples of the results of venery.

Fit to Fight had its effect, for a time, on the more impressionable of us. But not on Henry Macloy. When he returned to barracks that night I heard him announce that this was the most discouraging goddam war he had ever heard of. "Tryin' to take all the fun outa life," he said. He held the film to be nothing but mere fraud. Worse, even, he said, it was a low attempt on the part of the Y.M.C.A. to prevent honest girls from earning a living. To show what he thought of the whole business Mac promptly went AWOL for three days. When military police brought him back Mac told me that within fourteen days—the conventional danger period—he would prove to all and sundry that the sex film was a miserable hoax.

Apparently, Mac was immune to anything. When off duty, both in this country and abroad, he roamed and ranged everywhere, often to the lowest sort of dives. None of the evils shown in the film caught up with him. The flu epidemic was just so much good fun to him. Fleas and conventional lice never bothered him. Nor was he ever a member of our Blue Butter Squad which was troubled with *pediculis pubis*.

I got Macloy out of civilian jails in Boston, Lowell, and Fitchburg, Massachusetts, and out of a military jail at Winnal Down in England. Combinations of "drunk and disorderly" and "assault and battery" were the usual charges. The time Mac got into the jam at Clermont-Ferrand, in the Puy-de-Dôme of France, was probably the most serious.

Mac had gone on Sunday leave to Clermont—in order to attend high mass, he had said. Late that evening a telephone call came to battery headquarters from an excited French policeman. He jabbered something about an American *soldat* named "MacAloy" who was locked up in jail, and what was I going to do about it. My understanding of French, over a French telephone, wasn't very good but the Frog policeman made it clear that this pig of a corporal MacAloy was jugged and charged with what appeared to be rape, arson, murder, and treason against *la Patrie*. This sounded reasonable.

I asked the excited gendarme to hold the guillotine a little while, until I could get there. Then, I put two cartons of Piedmont cigarets into my pocket, and rode the tinpot trolley line into Clermont.

I found Mac, with a notable hangover, but quiet enough, in a real dungeon cell, the kind they have underground. The French chief of police was at first very severe with me; but I was France-broken. Presently this pig MacAloy was released to me and the chief had two cartons of *cigarettes américaines*.

"Now," I asked Mac on our way home, "what happened *this* time? Did somebody insult the Grand Old Flag, or the Artillery, or your Old Mother?"

"No, sergeant," he said, "it wasn't none of them things this time. It was jest that a gal made a indecent proposal to me." Such a statement coming from Mac was almost beyond belief, but I let him go ahead with his story.

It appeared Mac had arrived in Clermont in the morning, had attended mass, as planned, and while strolling down the Place de Jaude had been accosted—"accusted," he had it—by a young woman. They went to a hotel, and there, Mac vowed, she had made this indecent proposal. One thing led to another and Mac pushed the girl through the tall windows of the hotel room.

Clermont is a noble old town. It saw Vercingetorix defeat Caesar on the near-by plain. Napoleon trained his artillery there, and much history and strange doings have taken place within its walls. But it horrified and scandalized the good Auvergnats, homeward bound from church, to see a young woman dressed in a pair of stockings, and nothing else, come crashing through a window and fall to the sidewalk.

It was to the glory of French womanhood that the girl suffered only a fractured leg in the affair. Before Mac could get into his clothes the cops had taken him. "Them guys made an awful stink over nothin'," he told me. He seemed surprised that he should have been arrested. "You can never tell what these jeasley furriners will do," is the way he summed it up.

That was the last time, during the war, that Macloy got into jail. At the front he proved as reckless under fire as he had showed himself to be with wine and women. It never seemed to occur to him that some of that stuff the Germans were sending over might have his number on it. To show his contempt for German shelling, he would sometimes clap what he called his "Mister Mellon's Patent Aluminum Mess-kit" on his head when he lay down in his dugout. He would serve the guns forty-eight hours without relief or bellyaching. The more blood and mud and noise there were, the louder he would bellow obscene lumberjack songs—things like "Roll of Old Gingerbread Nine Inches Long" and "The Red Light Saloon." His voice sounded like that of a gigantic bull.

Mac was the strongest man in the battery, maybe in the regiment. It wasn't part of his job but it pleased him to pick up two 155-mm shells, each weighing ninety-eight pounds, and plod slowly yet easily up the steep path from the shell dump to the gun pits.

I said Mac never bellyached about doing a lot of hard work or taking a long chance. He never did. But there was one subject he was ever ready to horse about and that was the so-called Candy Issue.

Mac had read in the somewhat unduly optimistic *Stars & Stripes* that one pound of fine candy was being issued each and every week to every enlisted man in the A.E.F. Of course, nothing like that ever happened; nor did Mac care a whoop about candy. But the subject was a red rag to him and I wish the editors who printed the pretty little candy story could have heard

Macloy, between rounds of his 155-mm gun, giving one of his blistering and highly original dissertations on what he termed "the failure of the Army or the goddam lying of them newspapermen."

Candy or no candy, Mac was a hellion when there was work to be done. On the moonless night we moved into the Argonne, Mac, using a worthless issue ax, laid into the French timber (he called it "bushes") in the manner of the great Paul Bunyan, in order to clear a path for one of the big guns. I never saw such ax-work anywhere; the stuff went down like wheat. His one night's work was worth a D.S.C. or a Croix de Guerre. Mac had never heard of either.

Good as he was at work, Mac's greatest value to us was as a keeper-upper of morale. He was worth more than the combined forces of George Creel's department of misinformation, the K. of C., and the Salvation Army combined. A raconteur of rare parts, he knew how to keep the boys from thinking too much about gas and shells.

I have heard Mac in a soggy gun pit, the usual French drizzle coming down and Fokkers droning overhead, give a long lecture about a huge boa constrictor which some vague uncle of his had taken a liking to and had harbored in his Maine barn for several years. How a boa came to be in that part of the country wasn't clear. It was a fact though, Mac averred, that his uncle had come upon it suddenly one night in the stable, had befriended it and fed it a "good grade of timothy hay" until the year of the July snow, which killed all the grass. I forgot what became of the snake.

Mac's family would often be the topic of these lectures during nights when the shelling was heaviest. The only one that could be reported here concerned an Aunt Myrtle. "Aunt Mertie was a fine good-hearted woman," Mac would tell. "One of the best in the country. She never married. Once in a while she'd have a kid or so, but only in fun, an' she cared for 'em good. Some as claimed she poisoned her mother—who was my great-aunt and a fine woman, too—but I never believed it. I think th' old girl got holt on some Paris green by mistake. . . . You know, they have lots of Paris green around in Aroostook County on account of th' potato bugs. But you know how folks in a small place will talk. . . . Then, there was the time they arrested Aunt Mertie for plugging that Canuck barstard, Doc Pellissier. You mighta seen about it in the Boston papers. But the pitchers they printed of Aunt Mertie didn't look like her a-tall. . . . She was a good-lookin' woman."

It may not sound so hot on paper but to hear Mac tell it in the gun pits was enough to make you forget all about the Hindenburg Line, the German artillery, even the Candy Issue.

Perhaps Mac's finest lecture was in regard to an Army regulation which forbade an enlisted man to wear a white collar. This regulation, I understand, has since been rescinded, but in those days, and after the Armistice, it was enforced with vigor. It was, in fact, a greater crime for an enlisted varlet to be caught on leave with a white collar showing around his blouse top, than it was to break many of the Ninety-six Articles of War.

Mac didn't give a damn about this regulation, for he had never worn a white collar in his life; and he had managed to attract all the women he wanted without adding finery to his issue uniform. So, it must have been the principle of the thing. Anyhow, Mac had run across an obscure passage in Army Regulations which designated the clothing an enlisted man should— nay, must—wear when he is prepared for military burial. One of the items so designated was: 1 Collar, white.

In other words, as Mac took great care to point out to his audience, enlisted men might wear a white linen strip around their necks only when they were ready for planting in the ground, an occasion when a white collar would be useless, so far as the

wearer was concerned, for the attraction of impressionable fe-
males. "You see," Mac would say, "th' officers has got all you
guys on th' hip."

To the uninitiate this might sound like doctrine subversive to
the best Army discipline. Yet it wasn't. It tickled the few city
slickers we had; while as for the boys from the woods, no logger
of that day would stand for a white collar around his neck except
on those two state occasions when he was in no position to do
much about it, viz., at marriage and at death.

So, in recent years, when I read of some ex-soldier receiving
a Purple Heart or other decoration for something done in 1917–
1918, I think it would be swell to find ex-Corporal Henry Macloy
and to bestow recognition on him. He wouldn't know what to do
with a Purple Heart, but I'm sure, wherever he is, that he could
use a case of rye to good advantage.

Up the Fraser River, in British
Columbia, was the

Bughouse Camp

AFTER I got the job I went down to the
employment office on the skidroad and told the shark to forward
any mail for me in care of the Jesse James Jenson Logging Company at Big Creek.

"So you got the job at Jesse's?" he said. "Well, she's a bughouse camp proper."

I had just come for the first time to British Columbia after a
winter in the North New Hampshire woods. I wore a derby hat,
not uncommon with loggers when in town in the Northeast, but a
hat such as had not been seen on the North Pacific in many a
year. I think that at that time, in 1920, it was the only derby
hat in all the province. I had noticed people on the street looking at it. It got me the job anyway; I found that out the same
day I hired out. As I was riding up the Fraser River toward
camp with Jesse James Jenson himself, he remarked about my
bowler.

"I hadn't seen a hard hat like that in ten year, until you come
into the office. It tickled me."

That's how I got the job at what the shark had said was a
bughouse camp proper.

Jesse James Jenson was a stocky man, hard of face except
when he laughed. I afterward learned that he had come to British
Columbia from Minnesota, where he had worked in logging
camps ever since he was a youngster. He had lost two fingers

on his left hand somehow. His eyes were slaty blue. At the time
I first met him he was rated one of the largest and most successful logging operators in the province and by all odds the hardest-
boiled and most eccentric. He didn't talk much on the way to
camp.

After turning off the main highway we drove many miles over
a narrow road up a mountain. On both sides of the road as far
as we could see, there were stumps. Stumps, brush, weeds, thousands of feet of logs lying crisscross, and old snags. I had been
used to logged-off country all my life but never on such a scale
as this. It was complete desolation. I am no aesthete yet the
sight struck me forcibly. I said something about its being a pity.

"What's a pity?" Jesse barked.

"Why, all these ghosts of a fine forest," I replied, somewhat
poetically I suppose, and waved a hand at the miles of black
stumps.

"Did you say you was a logger or a forestation professor?"
he demanded, and went on in a softer tone, "It *is* a goddam pity;
but I ain't seen nobody yet what would pay me two-hunnerd
thousand for lettin' her stand. . . . That's what I got outa th'
logs."

We ran through several more miles of stumps and got to camp.
It was a large one, even for the Pacific Coast. The office and a
good-sized store made up one building. From there to the great
cookhouse stretched four long rows of bunkhouses. I had a shack
to myself. So did the camp foremen. There were a few families
in camp who had shacks to themselves also. In my years in the
Eastern woods I had never even pictured such a layout as this.
If it was a bughouse camp, it was a new sort to me, and I liked
the look of it. It *was* a good camp, too, only a little queer at
times.

My duties included handling the white payroll, doing first-aid
work, and helping with surveying when lines were to be run.

There were some two hundred whites on the payroll. Below the main camp was the China camp. Here lived about fifty Chinese who did the falling and bucking of timber.

One of the most important features of the white camp, I soon learned, was the bar in one end of the camp store. It was the only bar I have ever seen in a logging camp. We had a man who opened up fifteen minutes before breakfast in the morning, again at noon, and at night until lights out. On Sundays it was open all day.

Theoretically the camp store was the usual sort of commissary kept by the company to supply the simple, homely needs of loggers; snuff, tobacco, work clothing and the like; but much of the storekeeper's time at the Jenson camp was required in the serving of an unlabeled beer product which appeared on the bills of lading every Monday morning as 10 bbls. Bottled Foam. At that time British Columbia had not recovered from the Presbyterian Terror. A little hard liquor could be bought, legally, on prescription, and more was bootlegged at even higher prices, but that was all. This Bottled Foam, however, did very well. It was the most powerful beer I have ever sampled. It was no uncommon sight to see stolid Swede loggers guzzle a couple pints of it and then stump out of the camp bar humming "Vortland" aloud, a thing done by Swede loggers only when under the influence of acute patriotism, or alcohol, or both.

The vice president of the Jenson Logging Company happened to be president of the brewing concern which put up the 6 per cent Foam; and thus we had good strong beer on tap at all times instead of the slop sold legally at other camps. At that time, right after World War I, there was a great to-do among the proletariat concerning the curse of interlocking directorates; and I enjoyed jibing the especially class-conscious loggers about it, pointing out that they were blessed with this potent Bottled Foam because of the benevolent interlocking of Big Business.

The man who tended the bar was a fellow of imagination. He
rigged up a piece of iron pipe for a foot rail. He cut revealing
pictures of movie women from magazines and pasted them on
the wall. Jesse had thoughtfully provided a huge cash register
with a bell on it that sounded like a guthammer gong, beautifully deep and long pealing. There were dice cups, too, some
punchboards and a gaudy slot machine.

To stand outside in the camp street on a Saturday evening and
listen to the joint going full blast was to recall the Scollay
Square, Boston, of prewar days.

II

Men became scarce in the summer of 1920, yet the Jenson
camp always had a full crew. Strikes, caused by the churlishness
of arrogant lumberworker union organizers and the bullheaded-
ness of employers, closed many camps in the province, and
across the line in Washington and Idaho as well; but not the
Jenson outfit.

The proletariat were roaring in the fullness of their new
power. There had been a police strike in Boston, a general strike
in Winnipeg, and the Ole Hanson "revolution" in Seattle. British
Columbia was full of the One Big Union, similar in membership
and tactics to our own benevolent and protective order of the
I.W.W. Lumber was high. The great sawmills on the coast
whined day and night. Log prices went skyhooting.

So wild-eyed fanatics cavorted on the skidroads. Fat and often
damnably lazy bounders became traveling delegates for the
O.B.U. and sold copies of Joe Hill's Wobbly songbook. Loggers
whose former interest in economics had been confined chiefly to
the cost of overalls and Copenhagen snuff, suddenly took to
speaking casually of what Mr. Marx said to Mr. Engels. The
Red Dawn was just over the hump.

Few of the logging operators would allow a known delegate of the O.B.U. in their camps, much less permit a meeting of the order on camp property. From the One Big Union headquarters in Winnipeg the camps were flooded every day with lurid papers and pamphlets calling on the workers to arise and shake off their chains in seven languages. Most of this went into the barrel stoves of the camp offices without the operators asking the comrades anything about it.

But at Jesse's camp we harbored, and knew it, at least a dozen delegates or active members. Most of the crew were packing red cards. The O.B.U. secretary received his hot stuff direct and in good order from the camp post office and sold or gave away as many papers as he would. The comrades held meetings in the bunkhouses, with the Jenson Logging Company paying for the lights.

"Let 'em r'ar on their hine legs," Jesse said. "It'll do 'em good."

During the summer there was an agitation for a qualified first-aid man in every camp. I considered myself pretty good at this work but I had nothing tangible to prove it; so Jesse had me go down to Vancouver for a week end, where I took a couple of lessons, passed my examinations, and received an astounding certificate done in three colors and signed at St. John's Gate, Clerkenwell, London, E.C., by no less a white-collar man than "Devonshire, patron," himself. Since I had never received a diploma of any sort, this document gave me considerable pride. I nailed it in a conspicuous place on a wall of the first-aid room and always called a patient's attention to it before performing an operation on him with iodine or Epsom salts.

One time, I am sure, the certificate was of great professional aid to me. I was approaching the cookhouse for dinner one noon when there was a great uproar inside. Presently a big Finn logger came out the door on the lam. Right on his tail came the even bigger cook, a meat cleaver in his hand. He let fly with the cleaver. It missed the Finn by a yard and struck fair into the side of a bunkhouse about twenty feet away, where it split a board from top to bottom. The big Finn turned and drew his knife. They grappled and in the wild scuffle that followed the knife cut the main artery in the Finn's right arm.

He started to run up the camp street, squirting blood horribly. I followed, trying to catch him to bind him up, but he thought we were going to kill him. Three of us finally captured him and carted him, howling and fighting, to the first-aid parlor. He continued to fight until one of the gang, a fellow countryman, pointed to my impressive certificate on the wall and said something in Finnish. The face of the wounded man at once became soft, and he smiled. He was docile and even respectful while I bandaged the wound.

The bartender always tried to be helpful in serious cases like this one. He would come to the door and proffer a free pint of Bottled Foam to the ill or injured.

"It'll reg'late the bile an' ease the kidneys, so's you'll get well quick," was his stock professional remark.

III

The China camp, just below our own, was ever a curious thing to me. I had known that Chinese used to run laundries in Northern New England towns, when I was a youngster; and the Nick Carter weeklies I had read had proved that all Chinese were highbinders who did most of their work with hatchets. But that a Chinese could be and was a logger who used an ax and a saw was a fact hard for me to accept. Yet the Jenson fallers and buckers were Chinese.

The bull bucker of the China camp—which is to say, the boss man—was an old leather-faced fellow who had been on the

West Coast since before the anti-Chinese riots early in the century. We had him down on the payroll as Washington Duck, and
his was the only name. The others were grouped as so many
fallers and so many buckers at so much a day. Then there was
a "cook, $100 month." My instructions were not to bother to
check the Chinese to see how many were actually at work every
day, but to take the time that Duck turned in as correct. At the
end of the month I would send a check for the entire yellow payroll to a Chinese labor agency in Vancouver. I suppose the
agency gave some of the money to those that earned it.

The China cook was quite a politician. Often he would send
me a dish of fancy-cooked rice and duck. At Christmas time he
appeared at the office with a large bundle under his arm. "You
like for Clistmas," he said, and left. The bundle proved to be a
huge cake. On the frosting he had lettered, with his finger, I suppose, a large pink heart which inclosed the legend "WeLcome."
The cake, and its legend, were of far more comfort to my soul
than a self-styled Lumberjacks' sky pilot who made several
abortive attempts to hold prayer meetings in camp during Christmas week.

One night I lay in my bunk reading when a devilish noise
suddenly started at the China camp. I had often heard them making noises down there but this night it was louder and more of
it. Drums were being beaten and a wind instrument that sounded
like a he-goat seeking a nanny was played upon. At intervals
there would be a terrific crash of cymbals. Obviously something
big was stirring.

The next evening the noise was resumed and continued most
of the night. In the morning Duck came into the office, another
Chinese trailing behind. This fellow was wearing a filthy ban-
danna handkerchief over one eye.

"You look China boy eye," said Duck. "See if fix it."

The China boy's eye was beyond fixing; the eyeball hung

far down on his cheek. After much argument Duck admitted that the accident had taken place two, maybe three days before; a bent-over crosscut saw had jilpoked and one of the rakers had lifted out the eye. I complained to Duck because he had not reported the accident sooner.

"We try China medicine first but no good," he said. "Now we try you doctor."

So I knew what the noise had been about.

I sent the poor devil to Vancouver where he was given a glass eye, and $700 by the Workmen's Compensation Board. The one-eyed boy soon sailed for China.

"He always lucky man," Duck told me.

There was only one row at the China camp that summer, and, of course, no white devil ever knew what it was about. One day the son and daughter of the camp blacksmith, just youngsters, came into the office and told me to come quick, that something dreadful had happened. I followed them down a path that led from the China camp to the creek. Not far from the path was a headless body. Wrapped carefully in a Chinese newspaper, about four feet from the body, was the head of a Chinese man.

We left everything as we had found it and I telephoned the sheriff's office. After looking over the field the sheriff called the provincial police. Investigation of every Chinese in camp brought out the fact that not one of them had ever seen the dead man, heard of him or of any of his relatives, or knew how he came to be where he was without his head. In fact, they appeared to be surprised at the corpse's presence near their camp.

Nothing, of course, came of the investigation, even though a news item in a Vancouver daily cleverly pointed out that the affair "appeared not to have been a case of suicide."

Always on the West Coast, the China boys have been held to be economic enemies of the white man. Probably they are. Yet I know that in the fall of 1920 the Chinese, in the Jenson camp at least, proved that they knew more than the white loggers when it came to the scientific application of pure, unadulterated Marxism.

That fall prosperity took a sudden dive downward toward normalcy. Employers saw their chance. Help was overrunning the country and there were no jobs; so wages were slashed to the bone. In the Jenson camp the O.B.U. comrades bellowed. They bellowed in vain, although a few of the most radical of them quit in protest. These went to Vancouver and presently, for want of something better, found themselves in the soup line of the Salvation Army.

But not the China boys. When I notified old Duck of a 10 per cent cut in wages, he understood what was meant at once, without any of the usual "no savvee" business.

"All right," he said cheerfully. "China boy no care; we catch log all same."

They did. They catched the log, all right, but their output was uncannily exactly 10 per cent less than it had been before the 10 per cent wage cut. I complained, officially, about the falling off in the log scale.

"Timber get awful tough," Duck explained to me carefully. "She hard for China boy. Never see so hard timber."

Such fellows needed no Marx or Big Bill Haywood.

IV

An ancient Scot named Donaldson was the stump inspector in the district where the Jenson concern was cutting timber. That is, old Donal was employed by the Dominion government to take a look at us every so often and make sure we were stamping each and every log that went down to water with the official D.T. log brand. Jesse James Jenson held that this idea of stamping all government logs was something much to be desired but most

difficult of accomplishment. And it is true that, in the great rush
for logs at that time, a few million feet of them were possibly
overlooked and not branded. Anyway, the camp foreman and I
had instructions to see that old Donal was so well entertained
whenever he came to camp that he would never get out to the
logging works.

Getting old Donal drunk was no work for weak, cowardly
men. He scorned the powerful Bottled Foam. We would feed
him straight Scotch for an hour or so and then hand him a shot
of Demerara rum to tamp it down, as he put it. He was the only
Scot I ever knew whose burr did not thicken in proportion to
the amount of alcohol consumed. Grog worked the other way with
him. When he was quite sober he talked as though his mouth
were full of haggis. After about one imperial quart of Johnny
Walker had gone down the ways, he spoke something approaching English.

Ordinarily the foreman, who was most able at the business,
and I could hold Donal pretty close to the camp stove by generous application of hard liquor and by listening to his stories, not
one of which I ever completely understood. But one day he
heaved into camp and caught us short on supplies. All we had
was one short quart of Canadian Club, a drink considered potent
enough by most people, but which old Donal termed a nice sort
of wine. We fed him all of the Canadian Club, drinking nothing
but Bottled Foam ourselves, but it didn't seem to do much good.
In fact it didn't do *any* good. Donal insisted on going to the
woods. There he happened on six Jenson cars loaded high with
government logs on which, unfortunately, there were no brands.

Donal made a big noise about the unbranded logs. He threatened to shut us down, which he had the authority to do, and
shouted that he would lay the entire matter before the Crown,
or the Privy Council, or somebody like that. The foreman played
what cards he could. He threw his hat on the ground, cursed hor-

ribly, and told the chaser, whose job it was to stamp the logs, to go get his goddam time, roll his blankets, and fly to Jesus out of there. "I'll learn you dudes to sit on your behind and not brand these-a logs," the foreman bellowed. Next day, of course, the chaser went back to his job at two bits more a day.

Jesse James Jenson managed to fix up our mistake somehow, but he gave the foreman and me a going-over about it.

"If I can't depend on you fellers to entertain a gov'ment inspector same's he shoulda be," he said, "then, by God, I'll get a couple of Siwash squaws to run this layout."

A *Jap plane set the Oregon woods afire with the*

First Bomb

IF EVER the government sets up a marker on a certain spot back in the hills six miles east of the remote hamlet of Brookings, on the coast of southwest Oregon, it will be with good reason. Scarcely an American outside the West Coast states appears to remember, or even to have heard of, the extraordinary event that happened there, but the fact is that is where the continental United States was bombed for the first—and thus far only—time from an enemy plane.

There is no question about the bomb or its parentage. In order to satisfy my curiosity about it, and since I live in the region anyway, I not only went to see the bomb crater [in 1942] but I held parts of the bomb in my hands. I also talked with the men of the United States Forest Service who saw the plane from which the bomb was dropped, sighted the smoke from the blazes it started, and put the fires out before they had a chance to grow to dangerous proportions.

Shortly after six-fifteen on the morning of September 9, 1942, Howard Gardner, the forest service guard stationed on Mount Emily in the Siskiyou National Forest, near Brookings, heard a plane. The exhaust, Gardner thought, seemed labored; it had a sort of delayed-action sound, something like an echo. Presently he sighted the plane. It was tiny, the smallest he had ever seen, and it had extremely short wings. It was flying eastward at a very low altitude—so low that Gardner could see its solitary occupant in the cockpit. Gardner picked up his telephone and called the forest ranger at Gold Beach, a small town north of Brookings, where there was a ranger station; it was then 6:24 A.M. "One plane, type unknown," he reported, "flying low, seen east two miles, now circling." A moment later, as he hung up, the little plane completed its circle and began flying west, toward the sea. It eventually disappeared in that direction.

That was all, just then. Gardner, who lives in a small glass-sided cabin on the top of Mount Emily, went about his daily chores. He cooked and ate his breakfast, washed the dishes, tidied up his cabin, and returned to his job of watching the hundreds of square miles of dark-green forest below him. He saw the fog banks gradually move out of the canyons and drift westward to the sea, six miles away. He took wind, temperature, and humidity readings, all part of his daily routine, and at times he wondered about the odd sound of the tiny plane.

At 12:20 P.M., six hours after Gardner had seen the plane, he noticed a plume of smoke in the east. This was not surprising. A brief but heavy thunderstorm had swept that part of Oregon the night before, and Gardner thought, not unreasonably, that the smoke was coming from a "sleeper fire." Sleepers are a common sort of forest fire. They are caused most frequently by lightning, and they smolder for several hours in the wet woods before they start to burn in earnest, as the weather clears and the sun dries out the forest. Gardner sighted the smoke on his Osborn finder, calculated its position, and again called the ranger at Gold Beach. "A smoke," he said, using the customary forest service formula, "Township 40 South, Range 12 West, Section 22. That's all."

The ranger at Gold Beach, a veteran named Ed Marshall, who was in charge of that district of the Siskiyou National Forest, immediately called another lookout and asked for what foresters call a cross shot and, now that the smoke had been sighted from two angles, he was able to locate the fire with absolute accuracy on a map by triangulation. He phoned Gardner back and told him to go to the fire. It was 12:25 P.M. Marshall then dispatched three other foresters to the fire—Keith Johnson, Bob Larson, and Freddie Flynn. Two of these men were stationed at Gold Beach; the third had a post in the forest not far from Mount Emily. They had a fairly good trail almost to the fire, but when they arrived, bringing fire-fighting equipment, Gardner was already there.

Gardner's trek to the fire was made with a speed that is considered remarkable even by his fellow-woodsmen. From his station on Mount Emily to the spot designated as Township 40 South, Range 12 West, Section 22, is approximately four and a half miles cross-country. This particular four and a half miles of cross-country, in this wild part of Oregon, has to be seen— and walked over—to be believed. It is a jungle, a trackless forest of Douglas fir with a ground cover of devil clubs, chinquapin, and other difficult brush. The earth goes either uphill or down, the hills are high and the canyons deep, and there was no trail of any kind that Gardner could use. Nevertheless, he made the four and a half miles in three hours and thirty minutes, which will probably stand as an all-time record for the course. At 3:55 P.M. he was at the fire. Instead of a single blaze, he found several, some of which were burning briskly.

Long before they reached the scene, Gardner and the three other men all noticed what one of them described as an "ungodly stink." It was not, they agreed, the smoke of a forest fire, which is rather pleasant in its milder forms. Larson thought it smelled like burning rubber. Johnson said that the stench made him think of the odor from a carbide lamp. Flynn just didn't care.

When Gardner arrived, he noticed an oak tree which had been splintered and broken off as if by lightning. It was not burning. However, an old fir snag, dead and punky, was burning.

The other fires were all within a radius of a hundred feet from the splintered oak. Gardner went to work with ax and shovel, removing wood and brush from around the flames and throwing soil over them. Johnson, Larson, and Flynn arrived twenty minutes after Gardner and they, too, set to work. A little later Johnson came across a sizable hole in the ground. He thought it looked like a crater made by an explosion. "Hey," he called out, "somebody dropped a bomb here."

The others came over, thinking that Johnson was seeing things. The hole, however, certainly looked as if it had been made by a bomb and the stench from it was terrific. Johnson immediately hiked to the top of a nearby ridge, unslung the five-pound high-frequency radio that he carried as part of his equipment, and called Ranger Marshall, back at Gold Beach. He reported the fantastic news that the fire was not a sleeper but had been caused by an incendiary bomb, and returned to the fire. Looking around, he found fragments of evil-smelling, rubber-like stuff scattered over the ground. These were shaped like pieces of pie and each one had a small hole in it. "By God," he said, "there's enough stuff here to have set the whole of Curry County on fire."

The men paused for a few moments to inspect the fragments, then went to work on the fires again. By 8:20 P.M. they had them mopped up—not out, but under control and rapidly dying. Flynn, Gardner, and Larson left. Johnson remained to watch the fires and see that the last spark was put out.

Next morning, Les Colvill, assistant supervisor of the Siskiyou National Forest, and Marshall arrived at the scene. The old fir snag was still smoking, but the other fires were out. Colvill began digging in the hole with a shovel. The depression measured three feet in diameter and was eighteen inches deep. Presently Colvill's shovel struck something hard—a piece of metal that the three men were convinced had come from the nose of a

bomb. More digging uncovered a fuse head to which was attached a little fan that looked like a propeller. On the brass
collar of the fuse head were some minute markings.

All told, forty pounds of fragments were removed from the
crater and the area around it and taken to Brookings. An Army
ballistics man examined them and said that reclaimed rubber—
old American tires, perhaps—and thermite had been used in
making the bomb. The propeller fan on the fuse head had acti-
vated a powder train which burned down into the bomb, firing
its thermite-and-rubber center. A charge in the nose of the bomb
blew it apart when it hit the earth, scattering the fragments. The
Army expert said that the bomb had not been more than 40
per cent efficient, because it had been dropped from too low an
altitude to permit the powder train to finish its work. The markings on the fuse head, he said, were those of a certain Japanese
arsenal.

When I saw the bomb hole, it had been worked over, so I
couldn't tell much about its original appearance. I could see,
however, that the fires caused by the bomb had been so hot that
in some places around the crater the red clay earth had been
fused into lumps that looked like the flux from molten iron. The
wedge-shaped fragments, which I also examined, were still
smelly. After handling them, my hands retained the stench of
carbide, despite two good scrubbings.

A brief Associated Press dispatch, describing the bombing,
was sent from San Francisco on September 14th, five days after
the event. Then, buried under an avalanche of other and more
important news, the incident was forgotten. (Perhaps "forgotten" is not the right word. I failed to find anybody outside Cali-
fornia-Oregon-Washington, other than foresters, who ever heard
of the bombing of Curry County, Oregon.)

Except for the fact that the bomb had been dropped, however,
there was not much to get excited about, thanks to the prompt

action of the men of the forest service. All that the Japanese did, really, was to put another feather in the forest service's cap; and to give Township 40 South, Range 12 West, Section 22, the distinction of being the only piece of continental United States to have felt the impact of a bomb dropped by an enemy plane.

I t's a milder form
than it used to be, the

Lumberjacks' Saturday Night

A WAN December sun struggled briefly against the heavy clouds, then gave up, and the winter gloom of the Pacific Northwest settled down to bring night at four o'clock. All along the single street, the pavement began to gleam in the rain as one by one the neon signs came on in the score of false-front hotels, restaurants, stores and beer joints. Sifting through the leaky sides of the joints came the music of juke boxes, played by slugs furnished by the proprietors themselves, for Saturday night was coming to Chokertown and it has long been an axiom here that the joint with the most light and the most noise gets the business.

"Business" in Chokertown means loggers, lumberjacks. Less than half a mile from the High-Lead Hotel, in the center of town, begins the vast forest that runs almost uninterrupted for a hundred miles west to the Pacific shore and fifty miles east to the top of the high Cascade Range. It is a tremendous forest and here in the rain belt it is growing fast enough, so many foresters say, to keep Chokertown's loggers busy until the Round River freezes solid and alcohol and snuff drip copiously out of hemlock bark.

There, in an opening of this forest, stands Chokertown, already fifty years a lumber town but now getting a new lease on life as a place of entertainment also, a blow-in town, a whoopee place for lumberjacks.

Tire and gas rationing first brought Chokertown its new night life. It was really a revival, for, quarter of a century ago, Chokertown made lumber and also served as a place for loggers to blow her in. Then came the automobile and the good roads. Roads led right up to camp doors in the tall timber. No longer had a lumberjack to toil for six months without going to town to get his teeth fixed—as it is euphemistically termed. He could go to town every night in the week, if he wanted to. And he did. He spent a little but not much money, and returned to camp the same night. But this new-style lumberjack seldom went to Chokertown at all; he lit out for Seattle, for Aberdeen, for Bellingham—the big towns. So, small Chokertown kept on sawing the logs into lumber and lived a rather staid life. The great whoopee days had gone, never to return—or so most people thought—even though Chokertown's mills produced millions of feet of lumber every year.

Then, in 1940, began a demand for lumber the like of which had never been seen—lumber for cantonments, for hangars, for ships, lumber without end. Pearl Harbor set loose a new and greater demand which continued unabated through the war years and after. Prices hit the ceiling and so, finally, did wages in the woods.

Along came the tire menace. At first the loggers, like other folks, gave it little thought; but as old tires gave out, the logger found he would have to stay in camp nights, or walk—usually a matter of from twenty to forty miles. So the jacks stayed in camp, listening fitfully to the radio, or boredly to old-timers who liked to do some stove-logging. The younger jacks soon tired of such doings, for they were not accustomed to six months solid of camp life, or even six weeks of camp life, without a break. They pooled the surviving travel equipment—a couple of tires here, a couple more there, and a car—and ganged up for a trip to town on Saturday night. In many cases, it was not too difficult to persuade the bull of the woods, the logging boss, to run a train to town right after Saturday's whistle. It became a habit.

Look out, Chokertown, here we come!

So, last Saturday night, just as it has done on many Saturdays recently, the Two-Spot coupled up a mulligan car and a caboose at Camp Six of the Dosewallops Logging Company. The lokey's whistle let go a blast, and inside of two minutes, one hundred and forty loggers piled aboard. The Two-Spot's bell rang and she started with the train for Chokertown, twenty miles away.

We're the blue-eyed, bandy-legged, hump-backed old mackinaw hodags from Dosewallops!

Down, down the mountain, across high trestles, over dizzy canyons rolled the two carloads of lumberjacks, while the Two-Spot moaned and chugged, letting go a blast on the curves. Inside the swaying, bounding cars, young loggers shouted pleasant obscenities to each other. The lokey rattled on.

Look out, Chokertown, here we come! Eighty feet to the nearest limb and six foot through at the butt!

The Two-Spot's bell began to ring. The whistle sounded. The train crossed a switch with a clatter and ground to a stop at the log dump beside the river and less than twenty yards from the main street. Under blinking lights, the boys from the woods could see some of their handiwork—the log pond of the big sawmill filled with sticks, big ones, the stuff they had felled and bucked and sent to the saws. Under the lights, the pond men were still working, feeding the huge logs to the bullchain that took them up the curved slip and on to the whining bandsaws. Mills can work all night. Loggers can't.

II

In half an hour Chokertown was alive. I went to the High-Lead first and found the bar lined two deep, all drinking beer, the only drink served. The overflow stamped into Joe's Tavern and the Logger's Rest, two other beer places. A few of the more serious drinkers did not stop at all until they got to the State liquor store, where the State of Washington purveys hard stuff at rather high prices.

"No Liquor to be Consumed on the Premises," says a sign.

"Who the hell wants to?" It was Dan Peters, a tall and rugged hooktender from Dosewallops. With two pints of rye in his tin coat and two chokerman pals similarly rigged, the three headed direct for the Stockholm.

The Stockholm is not the fanciest place in town, but it has that something about it which attracts young and older loggers who take their fun as seriously as their work. Its modest neon sign, looking so modern and new against the false front of weatherbeaten boards, says simply that this is "The Stockholm, Good Food, Beer, Rooms." Inside, too, the Stockholm is a mixture of periods. It is one great room with a bar down one side, booths on another, food counter at the rear. In the exact center is a gigantic barrel stove, its pipe running nearly ten feet to the high ceiling, then ranging thirty feet through haywire loops to the rear wall. The floor between stove and lunch counter is broken only by one of the biggest and gaudiest juke boxes ever to come out of Chicago. It is lighted like Borealis and it fairly gleams and leers.

Above the bar, and hiking back to five-cent-beer days, is the conventional moth-eaten deer's head. Back of the bar stands Gus himself, the only bartender left in Chokertown with an indubitable walrus mustache. The bar gleams from polish. The glasses are piled in intricate patterns. A small framed sign contains a one-dollar bill and a historic notation: "First Dollar Taken Over This Bar, August 22, 1899."

"Hallo, falers" Gus greeted the arrivals. The booths already were filled with loggers, loggers and girls, guzzling beer or beer spiked with rye. The juke was hitting "Somebody Else is Taking My Place," loud enough to be heard above the alcoholic laughter. Half a dozen couples were on the floor. Not a mackinaw on the men, but all in conventional city clothes. Dan the hooktender and his pals sat down in a booth where four half-consumed glasses of beer still sat on the table. Just then, the juke ceased for a moment and two couples came to the booth. And right here marked, better than anything else could, the change that has come over lumberjacks. The two couples were strangers to Dan and his pals. They had obviously been occupying the booth. But no roughhouse ensued.

"Guess we took your booth," Dan said, starting to rise. "Sorry."

"That's all right," one of the strangers spoke up. "We can all squeeze in." They did too. The boys from Camp Six spiked everybody's beer. Turned out the other two lads were gyppo spruce loggers from the opposite side of the river. In a little while everything was rosy. Dan danced with one of the girls, and later took her upstairs to look at the stars. One of the gyppo loggers passed out and slid under the table, very quietly. Booze and bawds, maybe, but not battle. The lumberjacks' trinity has lost its third angle.

Over at the High-Lead, loggers still lined the bar and filled the booths, they and their girls. The juke box blared endlessly. I watched while men slid under tables, girls screamed beery laughter, or wept into their glasses; and one old battle-ax with a deep bourbon contralto stood up by the juke and sang "Good-bye, Little Darlin'" in a true and musical if husky voice, while a rigging slinger from Hamma Hamma, way to hell and gone over the other side of the hump, wept great tears and told me his girl didn't love him any more.

The odd thing is that nobody hit anybody. Nobody threw a beer

bottle. And those who might have looked closely at the husky contralto's hands could have seen calluses on them. For eight hours
that day she had been pulling lumber—boards to you—off the
chain in the mill across the river. She was but one of hundreds
of women who were lumberjacks for the duration, helping lumber
go to war and still working in a mill. And now a likely-looking lad
rushed over to the big contralto and filled her glass with whiskey.
She broke into her own song without benefit of the juke music:

> I'm a tearing old stiff full of slivers
> of Sitka,
> And I'm packing the wallop that
> went to beat Hit-la

"Amen, sister."

"Hold her, cutie, and watch that rigging."

The juke blared again and the dancers cavorted. The High-
Lead was shaking and shivering in every one of its old boards
and timbers. The proprietor told me it was going to be a one-
thousand-dollar evening, with no breakage except for possibly
a few beer glasses.

"No, sir," he told me, "loggers don't live in trees any more
and they won't necessarily eat hay if you sprinkle whiskey on
it."

In the Red Front Department Store across the street, a young
rigging man from Camp Six was ordering a copy of *Trees and
Forests of the Western United States,* by Hanzlik, a standard
work on forests. In another section of the same store ("We Sell
Everything") a high-climber from Hemlock Bay was buying a
whole list of stuff—for his wife back in camp; thread and didies
and a cord for the electric flatiron and such domestic things.

Mac's Barber Shop (four chairs) had a waiting line and many
of the boys were getting the works—shampoo and all—while a
Filipino lad shined their shoes, just as though they were city

slickers. The talk in the shop, I noted, was not about women and automobiles, but about log production.

Across from the barber shop I could see the windows and sign of Painless Prentice, the chain dentists. Four patients were in the chairs. This was the ultimate, the incredible—loggers coming to town to "get their teeth fixed" and actually going to a dentist! It almost passed belief.

One block away, down on the river bank, a row of three shacks represented all that was left of Chokertown's one-time full two blocks of cribs. In 1920, the cribs here numbered at least a score and they housed, so old-timers say, sixty women. Tonight, half a dozen women would entertain perhaps as many as twenty loggers, possibly thirty. This doesn't mean that morals have changed, for they never change. It means that many of today's loggers have wives, either in camp or in town.

<h2 style="text-align:center">III</h2>

I went back to my room at the High-Lead and there, over a few drinks, talked with a forester who had once been a lumberjack. Now he had charge of a forty-acre tree nursery owned and operated by a group of logging concerns.

"So loggers themselves are planting trees in these incredible times?" I asked.

"We'll plant about eight million this winter," he said matter-of-factly. "Beginning next season, about ten million a year. We raise them from seed at the Nisqually nursery."

"Did I understand correctly?" I asked. "Did you say that this nursery is owned and run by the logging operators themselves, the lumbermen?"

"That's right. And we can raise enough trees at Nisqually to plant every burned-over acre in Oregon and Washington. What is more, we *are* planting them."

I reflected on the late and terrific Jigger Jones, the old woods boss who swore that he wouldn't leave a tree standing between Bangor and Seattle, nor a virgin anywhere. The times were changing even more than I had thought.

At five minutes to midnight, the Two-Spot blew a blast and I went over to the siding to see how the boys had been making out. Perhaps a score of them showed signs of alcohol—in mild doses. Two were indisputably drunk, but moving under their own power. One was drunk *and* had a black eye. Only eight were missing and five of these were married men with wives in town. . . . In my days in the woods, I recalled, the only ones who would have been ready to return to camp at midnight would have been those who were carried. I watched the boys climb aboard. The bell rang and away went the hell-roarers of Camp Six, back to the timber.

One by one, the lights went out along Chokertown's main drag until only the High-Lead showed in the dark. I went in and talked with old Bill, the night clerk and chef, about lumberjacks old and new. "No," he said, "they don't kick out windows any more. But one'll kick hell out of more timber than the two of his grandpappies could. They're highball these days. Don't spend so much money in town. Nowhere near. Never throw money away, like it used to be. These boys going to get their money's worth. Hardly ever get to fighting. Jes' like to drink some beer, to dance them jitter things, play pinball machines."

I asked Bill if the young loggers were different in any other ways from the old-timers. He eyed me a moment, then spoke slowly and I thought sadly. "Well," he said, "they wear rayon underwear."

"That all?"

Bill turned his bloodhound's sad eyes on me. "No," he said, then lowered his voice as one does in speaking of some terrible infirmity. "They smoke cigarets and use talcum powder after they shave."

I went up to bed. Chokertown had gone to bed, too; that is, all except for the sawmill. I could hear the faint whine of its saws through the rainy night, and down on the pond I could see men poling logs to the ever-hungry slip. Four miles up the mountain, the Two-Spot sounded a last moan on her whistle as she headed up a ravine, carrying the boys who are better loggers and far shrewder playboys than their fathers were.

Y*ou never heard of John Turnow,
yet he was*

The Wildest Man of the West

IN THE Grays Harbor County court-
house at Montesano, in western Washington, a small bronze
plaque lists the names of six men and relates with sinister brev-
ity that they met their death in futile attempts to take the celebrated outlaw John Turnow. This is the only tangible reminder
of the most crafty and dangerous man ever to roam the timbered
reaches of the Pacific Northwest and by far the strangest outlaw I know of.

Through some incomprehensible literary freak, Turnow has
never been the subject of a paper-backed biography of the
Harry Tracy-Jesse James school, and the dime-novel trade thus
lost a sure-fire perennial. Hence Turnow's renown is purely local where it has flourished mightily for three decades and is in
no danger of dimming. Barrel-stove historians of the logging
camps, some of whom saw Turnow in the flesh and others of
whom were in at his death, keep the story alive and enhance it
with the embroidery characteristic of folk tales. When winter
gloom settles down over the still vast forests of the Olympic
Peninsula of western Washington and stiff gales make logging
operations dangerous, young loggers who have been brought up
on Tarzan and Superman sit on camp deacon seats and listen
with awed respect to stories of the life and times of a human
animal who combined in actuality many of the qualities of their
comic-strip heroes. In his own region, Turnow has long since be-

come a folk character comparable to the mythical Paul Bunyan.
And with some reason. The bare facts about Turnow were enough
to build a mountain of legend.

What might be called the public life of John Turnow began
on September 3, 1911, an otherwise pleasant enough autumn
day in the wild Grays Harbor country of western Washington.
A reddish sun beat down through the blue smoke haze of settlers'
clearing fires. Here and there in the vast wilderness the toot and
stutter of a logger's donkey engine could be heard. Blows of
firewood drifted like snow in the air and got into the sourdough
of the few trappers and prospectors in the region. Mostly,
though, the region was untracked, without roads or trails, and
silent except for the occasional bickering of jays and the report of some lone hunter's rifle.

On that particular September afternoon two rifle shots occurred, close together. If they were heard, no one paid them
heed or gave thought to the matter until it was learned that the
Bauer twins, John and Will, had not returned from a bear hunt
along the Satsop river. A few days later, Deputy Sheriff Colin
McKenzie, one of a large searching party, found the two bodies
tucked away under some brush, side by side, on the upper
reaches of the Satsop. Each had been shot once, and that through
the forehead.

John Turnow was at once suspected of the double murder,
strange enough when you knew that Turnow was blood uncle to
the twins, but not so strange if you knew about Turnow. This
man was thirty-two years old in 1911. Born of a pioneer and
respected family on the Turnow homestead near Satsop village,
John had never, people said, been quite right in the head. From
the time he began to walk he had been most peculiar. Didn't
care for human companionship at all. Wanted to be alone, especially alone in the woods. By the time he was ten John was
going into the timber along the Satsop and Wynooche rivers and

staying all night, sometimes for several days. His family tried to curb the youth's wildness, and his response was to stay away for a month. He told his parents that he found birds and animals better companions than men. He liked to listen to what he termed the talk of crows and jays, he said, and he also heard beautiful music, "like that of organs and harps" in the winds that sifted through the tall fir and hemlock.

On his lone trips into the woods young Turnow never carried any food. Got all the food he wanted from wild things, he said —roots, birds, animals. He always carried a rifle and when he was twelve he could drill a Copenhagen snuffbox at a hundred yards. At home he was moody. He did chores and other farm work under duress. He would not play with other children, not even with his brothers and sisters. I imagine he was what today would be called a retarded child.

So his parents finally sent John to a private sanitarium in Vancouver, Washington. Here he proved so hard to handle that he had to be removed and was then committed to an institution in Salem, Oregon. Though he was watched rather closely, one morning late in 1909 nurses found his bed empty. It hadn't been slept in.

Turnow left no connecting trail, but within a few weeks of his escape from Salem—which is nearly two hundred miles from the Satsop—trappers reported seeing him some twenty-five miles up the Satsop river. Turnow told two of these woodsmen that he would never be locked up again. He asked them to take a message out to his folks. "You tell them," he said in his short, gruff way, "and you tell everybody else that none of them had better come after me. I'll kill anyone who does. These are my woods. I want to be alone."

For almost two years Turnow lived on in the woods undisturbed, listening to those harps in the hemlocks, those arbor vitae organs, and communing with owls and cougars, a deranged and unlettered Thoreau without brains. His father died and word of it was taken to his son by a trapper who was on friendly or at least on speaking terms with him. John said he wouldn't go to the funeral, and he didn't; nor did he go a bit later when his mother died. The estate was left to the six Turnow children and John's share, some $1,700, was put in a Montesano bank and John notified by the friendly trapper. "I don't want no money," said John. He stayed on in the woods.

Such was the status of Turnow on that September day when his nephews, the Bauer twins, were found dead. It was surmised that the twins had been sighted by Turnow and that he may have thought they were searching for him, to take him back to the hated sanitarium. And Turnow, as was later to become very evident, was a man of direct action.

II

A huge man hunt followed immediately on discovery of the murdered twins. Some two hundred men ranged the Satsop and Wynooche watersheds for forty miles north and south, then spread east and west from Puget Sound to the Pacific. Here and there they found where the wild fellow had made camp, but not once was he sighted although the hunt was kept up sporadically throughout the winter of 1911–1912.

Meanwhile, the usual alarms occurred: Turnow was reported to be near Port Angeles. An unknown had killed a cow near Shelton. Another unknown who, by the size of his monstrous tracks in the snow, must have been huge, was said to be in the neighborhood of Hama Hama, on Hood Canal. Any or all of these reports may have been true. Turnow was now a man six feet two inches tall and he weighed around 195 pounds, all of it bone and muscle. He knew the woods of all western Washington as other people know their living rooms—and indeed these woods were John Turnow's living room. He traveled through the timber, hunters said, swiftly and with no more noise than the soft whish of an owl. And after a fresh fall of snow, at a time when the posses were thick and numerous, he left no tracks at all, leaving one to suppose that he holed up for weeks on end like a bear; or, as some said, he took to the trees.

In fact, one Emil Swanson, a log bucker of stout back and of no imagination whatever, came into a camp one night in a condition bordering on hysteria. Not until he had downed a lusty slug of high-power lemon extract in hot water could he compose himself sufficiently to say what was the matter. When he had been about to fell a big fir, he vowed, "some kind big animal, look like man," swung out on a high branch of the tree, grabbed the limb of another tree and went sailing off to be lost in the gloom of the towering timber. "Bay Yesus," said Emil, "aye vork here no more." He got his time and went to town.

The search for Turnow ebbed and flowed throughout the winter. Then, on March 2, 1912, word came out with a prospector that Turnow had made camp at a bend of the river far up the Satsop known as the Oxbow. Colin McKenzie, the deputy sheriff who found the Bauer twins, and A. V. Elmer, deputy game warden, started in to the Oxbow country to get Turnow. They did not return.

Thirteen days later a searching party found the bodies of the two missing men. Each had been drilled once through the forehead, and an attempt made to bury them in a shallow trench dug in the form of a T. Most of the dead men's clothing had been removed. Their rifles and ammunition were gone.

The hunt for Turnow now engaged the authorities of three counties. Rewards for the man, dead or alive, totaled $5,000, and hundreds of citizens joined the hunt. Not since the time of Harry Tracy and Dave Merrill had a man hunt of such proportions been on. The searchers used caution, too, for they knew they were pitted against a half-human animal who not only was deranged but who knew almost every acre of the large territory he had chosen for his home.

The usual alarms again occurred; the Wild Man of the Olympics, as the press now called him, was reported seen simultaneously in widely separated places. Loggers at the Simpson camps, nearly in the center of the region most favored by Turnow, took pains not to be found strolling quietly and alone through the woods. Southwest Washington, and in fact a good part of the Olympic Peninsula, had the Turnow jitters.

If you didn't know the country of John Turnow you might think it odd that more than twelve hundred men, most of them expert woodsmen, failed so much as to get sight of the wild man in a year's time of hunting. But Turnow had the craftiness of a cougar, and his domain was wide and wild. In 1912 it was pretty much virgin timber, not pines of parklike aspect, but a dense jungle of tall fir and cedar and spruce and hemlock, growing close together and with their bases set in vines and underbrush of almost tropical lushness.

Somewhere in that savage country the wild man spent the winter of 1912–1913, seen by no one. Not a track of his was found. Spring came on and the manhunt continued without abating. On April 16, 1913, almost two years after the murder of the Bauer twins, and more than a year after the killing of McKenzie and Elmer, Deputy Giles Quimby sighted a small wickiup, or rude shelter of bark, in a natural clearing by a tiny lake, perhaps a mile from the scene of the last two killings.

With Quimby were two trappers, Louis Blair and Charles Lathrop, who had turned man hunters with the $5,000 reward in mind. The three men were certain they had stumbled onto a hiding place of the wild man. But was Turnow there, in the hut? They withdrew to a safe distance to consider the matter; and after a brief council of war decided to approach the hut from three directions. They began the advance, slowly, cautiously, and as quietly, or almost as quietly, as a cougar stalking a deer, their rifles cocked. It wasn't, however, quiet enough. . . .

Deputy Quimby was moving ahead a few feet at a time, picking his every step and halting now and then to listen. He heard nothing at all until a blast of gunfire suddenly shattered the wooded silence. At the same instant he heard the crashing of brush and looked to see Louis Blair tumble headlong, blood gushing horribly from what had been his face.

Quimby's gun was at his shoulder. For a flash he saw a great head and an ugly bearded face pop out from behind a fir. Quimby fired. The head disappeared. Quimby knew the head belonged to John Turnow—but had he hit it with his shot? Quimby couldn't know—for a few moments. He listened, straining every sense to penetrate the deathly silence. Then came another shattering blast. Charles Lathrop threw up his arms, gave one agonized cry and went tumbling to the ground. Again the ugly head and face peered from behind the fir tree. Quimby fired instantly, again and again, until his gun was empty. He crouched down to reload. He knew he was alone now with the wild man.

With his rifle once more ready, Quimby peered around the tree he was using for protection. He saw that his tree had been chipped by bullets and knew then that Turnow had also been shooting at him, though Quimby had been too busy to notice. He looked at the tree where Turnow was hiding and could see that it had been chipped by his own bullets. But, and it was rather important to know, had one of his bullets hit Turnow?

Deputy Quimby couldn't know. He pondered. All was silent in and around the glade. That is, silent except for the worried sniffing of two hounds belonging to Blair and Lathrop. Quimby could hear the animals whining in wonder at the sudden smell and aspect of Death. But of Blair or Lathrop or Turnow, Quimby could hear nothing. For probably five minutes, which Quimby later declared to have seemed an age, the deputy listened. Then, as quietly as he could he made his slow way through the timber and away from the lake. It had been an ambuscade, and for all he knew it might be one now. When he had got a hundred yards or so from the spot Quimby stopped to listen again. The mournful baying of the two hounds, still contemplating their late masters, was all he could hear. He now put on all speed and hurried to Camp 5 of the Simpson Logging Company, four miles distant. Here he found High Sheriff Matthews with a large posse. He led them back to the sinister little lake.

All was quiet. The posse spread out, then converged slowly toward the wickiup. Presently came a shout. "Here's the son of a bitch," a deputy called. "And he's dead, by God." At about the same time other posse members found the bodies of the two trappers. Each had been shot once, fair between the eyes.

III

John Turnow hadn't been shot through the head, but he was just as dead as the six men he had killed. There he was, the wild fellow, sprawled on his back, his big old-fashioned repeating rifle across his chest and clutched in his two hands. He was a sight that men who saw him vividly remember today, more than thirty years after. The huge wild man with great matted beard and long hair, dressed in ragged garments made chiefly from gunny sacking, laid fold upon fold and filled with fir needles. On his feet was the only conventional bit of clothing he possessed, a pair of comparatively new calked boots, later identified as having belonged to the late Colin McKenzie, one of Turnow's victims.

In the little hut by the lake the posse found $6.65 in silver, a small knife, a pair of scissors and more gunny sacking of the sort the wild man had used to make his clothing. Not in the hut or anywhere else in the vicinity could the posse find so much as a scrap of food.

Reconstructing the brief, deadly battle, it was thought that Turnow, who had been accustomed to meeting *pairs* of men in the woods, and killing them, had not at first suspected the presence of a third man. It was a bullet from Quimby's gun which killed the outlaw.

Horses were brought in and Turnow and his last two victims taken out to Montesano, where an undertaker said he had never before seen the like of Turnow—all of the big man was bone and muscle. His shoulders, so the mortician reported, were like those of a gorilla; the palms of his hands were like leather. From this report, perhaps, and the added fact that it had never been possible to trail Thurnow—either in snow or on bare ground— plus the experience of Emil Swanson, he who saw the strange thing among the treetops, grew up the story, still widely believed, that the wild man often traveled through the trees, two hundred feet above the ground, like a gigantic ape. Perhaps he did. In any case, he went straight into legend, and there he remains today, half man, half ape, the Wild Man of the Olympics, intimate of bear, cougar, owls and buzzards, an unlettered, witless Thoreau who wanted to be alone and worked hard to that purpose.

*They would make you believe
that they eat nails—*

Whistle Punks

WHEN I first went to work in a logging camp in the Pacific Northwest and heard mention of "whistle punks" I thought the term had reference to some mythical animal like the swamp wogglers and side-hill badgers of the East, or to some fabulous character of the Oregon timber. But I soon learned that whistle punks were very real, and very, very hardboiled.

In the West any boy is known as a "punk," just why I haven't learned. Whistle punks are officially known on camp pay rolls as signal boys. They are the youthful loggers who, with jerk wire or electric toots-ee, give the signals for starting and stopping to engineers of donkey engines that yard the big Douglas fir timber, up and down the West Coast. They are automatons, standing throughout the day in one spot and yanking the whistle wire once, twice, or in combinations, in answer to the hook tender's orders. The hook tender has a log ready. He shouts "Hi!" The punk jerks his whistle line and the whistle on the engine snorts. The engineer "opens her up," and the log is brought in to the landing.

Despite his lowly job, which compares in dignity with that of the water boy of construction gangs, the punk is a well-known character in the Northwest. In Tacoma, Washington, the "Lumber Capital of America," a newspaper used to have a daily column headed "The Whistle Punk." I hold the punk to be well worth a column.

225

When placed alongside the average whistle punk, the so-called tough kids of the Bowery and the gamins of Paris are like so many cherubim. Punks are the hardest kids ever; or, at least, they *want* to be. They are so tough they won't even read the *Police Gazette*. To hear one talk you would suspect that he liked for breakfast nothing so much as a keg of iron bolts soaked in gasoline, wood alcohol, and snuff.

The vizor of the punk's cap is worn smooth where it has rested over an ear. His best Sunday conversation sounds like extracts from Rabelais; and when he is going *good* he can outcurse any cockney that ever mentioned the King of England. When he spits, it is what learned men term a cosmic disturbance. . . . Yes, the punk is *hard*.

The toughness of the punk is equaled only by his bellicose precocity. He is what an Englishman calls "a little bounder." Although he is but eighteen years of age, the punk often calls the camp foreman "boy" and gets away with it. When the foreman has occasion to bawl out the rigging crew, the punk adds a caustic razzing: "Who tol' you guys you was loggers?" Of an evening when some of the old-timers are doing a bit of stovelogging around the big heater in the bunkhouse, the punk horns in with some of *his* experiences. And his talk, when they will let him talk or when they cannot prevent him, is well interspersed with those short but expressive old Anglo-Saxon words of less than five letters. The subject of his logging tales is always the same: how he told the hook tender to "go to hell," or the timekeeper to "make 'er out, damn her." I have heard twenty-odd different punks tell exactly the same story in precisely the same words, and I am forced to the conclusion that the formula has been secretly published and circulated among them.

As a gambler the punk believes himself the genuine, one-hundred-dred-proof Hoyle. He is the kind of wise youth who tells the world he knows when to play 'em and when to lay 'em down.

But he seldom has enough money to interest the camp tinhorns; otherwise someone would have to write a new song about the punk who broke the bank at Monte Carlo.

The punk's literary tastes are simple. He likes *The James Boys in Missouri* and *The Life and Battles of John L. Sullivan.* In his suitcase he has a pamphlet clandestinely purchased from a news agent on a railroad train. It concerns the life and works of a frail yet beautiful lady known as Mayme, no last name given. It was never entered at the post office as second-class or other matter. He also reads the "comic books." Occasionally he will, in a blatant voice, read aloud the asininities of that popular family of morons answering to the names of "Min" and "Andy."

It is the camp cook, more often than not, who removes some of the offensive freshness of the punk.

This camp chef is the master of all he surveys. The kitchen and dining room are his precincts, and he guards them no less jealously than he does his dignity as cook. He is supreme monarch of the mulligan. Loud, boisterous talk from the crew at mealtime, to the cook's way of thinking, should be punished by no less an operation than speedy decapitation; while derogatory remarks about the fare, or in fact any sort of wisecracks around the cookhouse, call for complete annihilation. Thus it is the cookshack where the forward-looking punk often meets his Waterloo.

Once at a camp on the mighty Fraser River in British Columbia, I witnessed—and cheered on—the freshest punk that ever blew whistle being propelled suddenly, openly, and manifestly from the cookhouse door, and to a distance of some twenty feet beyond, all by the honest right boot of one Erickson, a noted camp chef of the time. The punk was not only booted clear of the hallowed precincts, but with him at the moment were at least ten million vitamins, in the form of bread dough, plastered well over his head and running down both cheeks, thrown there, as I later learned, by Chef Erickson. Inquiry brought to light that the

punk, in his usual carefree way, had wandered into the kitchen
where Erickson was making bread, and had asked him, brightly,
why it was that Danes were so much smarter than Swedes. Erickson, it appeared, had been born in one of the Faubourgs of Stockholm.

The punk's private idea of heaven is to have a trick suit of
clothes with two-toned coat, a long haircut, a chick, at least $15
in his pocket, and an old car stripped of all but its lungs and
rigged up to look as the punk thinks a Mercedes racer looks.
Here is paradise enow!

But he can't have heaven and his $7.00 a day at the same time,
and so when in camp the punk does the best he can with cigarets,
snuff, chewing-tobacco, and loud talk. This snuff is not the kind
that our forefathers sniffed. It is a powerful concoction of finely
ground tobacco known as Scandinavian Dynamite and is carried
in the lip. It is the badge of the he-man.

Just plain snuff, however, is not enough for the punk who
is really *hard*. Not at all. He first fills his lower lip with the snuff
and then wads in a bite of plug-tobacco. On Sundays he does
even better, when, in addition to this monumental chew, he simultaneously smokes a cig'ret. It is here he rises to heights of *he*.
He blows smoke out of his nose and mouth, and if it were possible he would blow it forth from his eyes and both ears. If a
punk ever succeeds in accomplishing this latter feat, he will become the greatest punk of all time.

The punk's boots always have the longest and sharpest calks
in the camp. If calks were made six inches long, the punk would
have them. How he loves to stagger carelessly into the bunkhouse,
stand still a moment until he gets his calks well set into the floor,
and then turn sharply on his heels in an effort to rip the flooring
asunder. No really good punk stops short of a two-foot splinter.

Some can split an inch board. Hard? . . . If they ever build bunkhouses with cement floors whistle punks will quit cold.

When a punk stags (cuts off) his pants legs, he stags them four inches higher than any one else in camp. When he paints his slicker to keep out the rain, he paints it *red!* His bunk is the dirtiest on the claim. The cuspidor besides his bunk is a keg, sawed in two.

In all these things the punk is colossally he. But there is another side to the story of this most masculine youth, for, like all red-blooded men, he has a weakness. *It is chocolate bars.* Yes, sir, a weakness for those bars of candy so popular with children and young ladies. The choc'lit bar is his one vulnerable spot. One minute he may be telling how he would like a good meal of canned heat, or making a cynical reference to the origin and forebears of the camp foreman; but expose him to a soft brown bar of chocolate, and you have taken the wind from his sail. He is half ashamed to take it, but he is helpless.

On an average it requires six choc'lit bars daily to run a punk, with ten on Sundays. It is here that he falls down in the business of being a tough guy. For whoever heard of a tough guy, a real he-logger, eating choc'lit bars? It is preposterous. And the punk feels it. But what would you? . . . Youth must be served, and no man can rise above his eighteen years.

So, when in camp I used to tire of the punk's heavy-duty stories and tough tales and loud blats and cursing and cynical jeers, why, I would just reach out right in front of the whole crowd and offer him a chocolate bar. I called it by name, so that all might see and hear: "Hey, punk, want a chocolate bar?" He would waver a moment between acceptance and scornful refusal . . . but the choc'lit bar always won. This shamed and tamed him for the evening at least; he would munch his chocolate and remain quiet.

It was worth ten cents.

There They Stand, the Yankees

IT WOULD be a bold man who would make a flat and inclusive statement as to what New England Yankees think of the rest of the country—bold, and as ignorant of the subject as a yearling bull in the remotest pasture of Coös County, New Hampshire.

Yankees are calm people, at least outwardly, and also are doubtless as opinionated a folk as can be found north of the Mason and Dixon line. But their opinions are very complex, are more often felt than spoken and are never dramatized.

Shortly after the hurricane of September, 1938, I spent a week in the devastated areas of Massachusetts, Vermont and New Hampshire. Timber of pulpwood size—an important cash crop in New England—was strewn everywhere. I talked with farmers, owners of the windfalls. One felt "the gov'ment" ought to come right out to his place at once, log the felled timber and pay him a spanking good market price. I talked with fourteen others. Without exception they didn't want any "gov'ment monkey business" at all; they felt they had the situation well in hand.

None of these men, all of whom had been hard hit, felt in the least sorry for himself. A few did curse mildly at Providence, if that was who "sent this goddam wind," and one seemed to think the wind itself had somehow been the result of machinations on the part of the current [Democratic] administration in Washington.

Of dramatics there was none. Here was the almightiest wind

Copyright, 1941, by Stewart H. Holbrook. Originally published in *The American Scholar*.

to hit New England since old William Bradford recorded the big one of 1635. Death and destruction had been on a scale almost the equivalent of that in San Francisco's quake and fire, but you would not have guessed it from anything the Yankees said. Typical, and more amusing than most, was the comment of a friend of mine, an old-line Yankee of Vermont. He and I walked out to his sugar place to view the seven hundred old maples that had been blown down. I tried to think of something appropriate to say but the best I could manage was an inane remark about its having been a big wind. My friend eyed the maples he had known since boyhood, now useless as sap-makers. Then he spat contemplatively. "Well," he said, "she wa'n't no zephyr." He then told me he was trying to figure whether to put the wrecked sugar place into cordwood or attempt to sell it as pulpwood. He hadn't even thought of assistance, from "gov'ment" or anyone else.

Well, there they stand, the Yankees. This spirit of independence is thinner in New England than it used to be even thirty years ago. Perhaps it is thinner everywhere in the United States. But the genuine Yankees are still the toughest-minded people we have and it is this spirit that influences much of their point of view and their relations with the rest of the United States. It is responsible for most of the Yankee's admirable characteristics and for practically all of his faults and shortcomings.

As a whole the Yankee envies no people of any part of our country or of the world. True, he likes to complain about his weather and if he is able he may run down to Florida for a few months in the winter. But Florida to him is nothing but a rather interesting and pleasant three-ring circus where it doesn't snow. He couldn't imagine anyone *wanting* to live there.

Yankee farmers work some of the toughest lands on the face of the earth. They hear about the rich soil and "easy" one-crop farms of the West. One of them may read that the Government pays billions of dollars in subsidies to Western farmers as well as to those in the South and he is mystified and a little dazed that such things can happen. Heavy sugar like that never came his way. Deep in his heart he doesn't want it to. Deep in his heart he thinks Government subsidies, like the W.P.A. and other new-fangled economies, are high-falutin' names for plain charity.

"We still got poor farms,* ain't we?" one Yankee said to me. "Then why in thunder don't we use 'em?"

That sort of thinking is "antiquated" in other parts of the country—a horse and buggy attitude. Perhaps it is. In any case I am not defending it. I simply want to make clear that that is exactly what hundreds, and for all I know thousands, of Yankees are thinking. It displays, too, another Yankee characteristic—his healthy distrust of euphemism.

The late Calvin Coolidge will scarcely be remembered for anything he did as President but he made one deathless remark. When asked about the possibility of easing the large debt of a foreign power to the United States he said, "They hired the money, didn't they?" In other words, the Yankee doesn't think that anyone, he or another, should get what he considers something for nothing. Extenuating circumstances? "That's another name for poor judgment." This may be, probably is, an admirable quality but it makes for hardness. Not for nothing was the main villain of many an old-time melodrama a Boston banker. Still, there are few safer places for a widow's savings than a New England bank.

Smugness probably stems from the same source and that source is without question a feeling of self-righteousness. In varying degrees Yankees *are* smug. This smugness cannot be better illustrated than in most of Boston's stores and other places of business. It is very doubtful that worse salespeople are to be found than in the Hub's big department stores. You can, if you

* County-operated farms for the indigent.

persist in spite of a vast disinterest, manage to buy something; but you will most assuredly learn that the stuffy person behind the counter isn't going even to simulate interest in you or in what you want. If it is granted that these underlings only reflect the attitude of their employers, then Boston's mercantile captains are smug also.

The Yankee's brand of smugness is more noticeable in Boston than elsewhere in New England only because it is concentrated. It prevails in all six states, in urban and rural districts alike. It is likely, too, that some of the stuffiness in New England business and social contacts stems from a genuine shyness, a dread of seeming "forward," carried to ridiculous extremes. And because of this ingrained smugness and shyness the Yankee fails to respond socially as do people in parts West and South.

This makes for a real if subconscious feeling of isolation, and the feeling is heightened of late years because the Yankee of old-line stock is currently a minority in almost every section of what was once his domain. Beginning with the Irish immigration of almost a century ago and continuing down to the most recent arrivals of Poles and Finns and Italians, New England's racial mixture has increased steadily.

The birth rate of the old-time Yankee has declined; and Yankees have left New England by the hundreds of thousands. You will find them or their second- and third-generation descendants all the way from the Western Reserve to the ends of the Oregon Trail, where old Yankee family names are prominent in cities named, like Portland, Oregon, for familiar places.

This immigration and emigration have had a powerful effect on the Yankee who still lives at home. They have made him a minority in his native region. He has not, however, reacted to his situation in the manner of most minorities. I have yet to hear the cry of persecution from him, the howl of "unfair competition" or of envy. He may be no longer a dominating character, in the mass; but individually he is still tough in body and mind, probably as self-reliant a person as were his ancestors of Colonial and Revolutionary times.

But his toughness is now defensive, made so by the conditions he faces. Economically he has never known really "good times." If there was ever a boom era in New England it occurred before my grandfather was born in 1836. That is why Yankees are parsimonious when there is no need for parsimony. It is the result of what some learned man termed "accumulated memory." You do not yourself have to recall, in person, three centuries of toil and sparse living. If you are a Yankee it is born in you just as the color of your eyes is determined.

That is why New England considers the rest of the United States profligate—including its Federal Government. That is why per capita savings in New England increased even during depression years and why they are and always have been the highest per capita savings in the country. Back of it is the folk memory of the Erie Canal which first depopulated New England farms and villages and played havoc with all Yankee economy. Back of it is folk memory of grim climate and poor soil which, even in New England's rural heyday, called for backbreaking work and careful use of food and clothing. Back of it is memory of the loss of many industries.

I have Western friends who have visited New England. They have first of all noticed the stuffiness, the lack of spontaneity in casual contacts, the careful, almost cautious overtures—if they could be called that—toward acquaintance or friendship. Next, my Western friends have noted parsimony—apparently well-to-do men carrying on business in shabby offices, with antiquated equipment, with their wives going out to dinner in old and dowdy clothes. "Is this a pose?" my friends have asked. It isn't a pose. It is the result of that accumulation of folk memory, a habit of

making things do until they won't do any longer. Ben Franklin,
or rather Poor Richard, would approve of it.

But this parsimony, plus an almost pathological resistance to
change, has been fatal to a lot of New England industry and
business. The directors of the great mills of Amoskeag, New
Hampshire, for example, were fond of old machinery that had
seen half a century of service and was therefore, according to
best Yankee traditions, the kind of machinery to keep; and
Amoskeag's directors continued to believe, until the bitter end,
that print and gingham were just what American women would
always want. They thought rayon and other new fabrics were
just a rumor. In parts of New England it is still difficult to sell
farming machinery driven by diesel or gasoline engines. Yankees
are going to wait until they are sure "it has come to stay." This
is by no means general but it is most typical of old Yankees and
has a bearing on the way they look at the United States.

The United States to them is a great, good and powerful
country of which they are the essence—or rather they consider
the United States to be the essence of Yankees that has flowed
out of New England and spread to the Pacific Coast, hewing
down the forests, building towns and cities, founding churches,
schools, colleges and business houses, all to the great glory of
the United States and to the local detriment of New England. By
and large an eloquent Yankee can make out a pretty good case
for this thesis.

That neither New England nor its people and works are so
important to the United States today as they were to the United
States a century ago goes without saying. The country has grown
since 1840. But the Yankee shows little or no resentment. He is,
in spite of millions of words to the contrary, basically a very
tolerant man—I think the most tolerant in the Republic. His
private opinion of the Social Security Act may be unprintable.
(Social Security to *him* is spending less than he earns and keep-

ing the haymow and cellar filled.) His pronouncements on the rising public debt (previous to defense spending) would not do in the mails. He doesn't think much of the Federal Government's building dams and going into public utilities (in Vermont men took shotguns in 1938 and threatened Army engineers who had designs on a local river).

But if the majority of Americans want those things—well, he won't carry a banner against them.

In matters of geography the untraveled Yankee knows, in a general way, that the United States is bounded on the West by the Pacific Ocean. He may have read an article about current events in the South, the Midwest, the Far West. He may even attempt to show interest in those events. Down deep, however, he doesn't care in the least. His physical world is pretty much bounded on the west by Lake Champlain and the Hoosac Tunnel. What goes on in the foreign parts beyond may sometimes be interesting or amusing but is hardly important to his life and times.

At home, however, he is alert to all the issues of the day, extremely well posted on matters that may affect him directly. So far as local affairs are concerned he is the best citizen in the country. Because of his system of town government, with its annual town meeting, he is civically very conscious, considering it an honor to be elected town selectman and a duty to do the job well. The smaller New England communities get more good government for the dollar than any other places I know of. So the Yankee wonders dazedly at the apparently endless forms the Federal Government takes. If he can run his community without a lot of furbelows what's the matter with the rest of the country that it needs nursing along by all the alphabetical bureaus? Given a good Army and Navy, the Yankee feels he can take care of himself and his own and that the other parts of the Republic should do the same.

Dr. Claude M. Fuess, retired headmaster of Phillips Academy at Andover, Massachusetts, was quoted as saying that Yankees are too isolated and are becoming "pathetic figures, furtive and even desperate, who dread the competition of everyday normal life." This is an absurd statement, but can be excused because although he has lived in New England for many years Dr. Fuess is really no better than a foreigner since he was born in Waterville, New York—which is halfway to Buffalo, which in turn, to real Yankee thinking, is right on the border of Outer Mongolia.

No doubt there are Yankees who are pathetic and furtive and even desperate, but not very many. Only the Mormons have equal or comparative backbone and the Mormons have their church to lean on whereas Yankees, in the memory of living men, have not leaned on any church and amazingly little on any government.

And when it comes to "the competition of everyday normal life" I shouldn't like to face competition any greater than that confronting the average Yankee farmer and villager every morning as he arises at six or earlier in order to make both ends meet. In spite of this competition, which the Yankee has known for more than a century, he remains basically a genial man with a sense of humor—which is to say a sense of proportion—and a sense of dignity, two of the most valuable things any civilization can have.

Dr. Fuess, whom the late and profane Ethan Allen would doubtless have referred to as a damnable Yorker, is on firmer ground when he observes that the Yankee is slowly but surely disappearing. So he is and I know of no way to preserve him. Dr. Fuess thinks he should intermarry with central European immigrants and thus "regenerate the species." I think it is all right for him to intermarry with central Europeans, or with Laplanders. But this would not preserve the Yankee. The resulting strain might be, as Dr. Fuess believes and hopes, a better race. So it might, but it would not be Yankee. It might not be half Yankee or even one third.

I judge that in time the old-line Yankee will wholly disappear. His families become smaller with every generation. Death and migration continue to thin his ranks and the movement toward extinction will doubtless go on. In another century, or two perhaps, it will be impossible to discover an American who uses an "r" in words without that letter and who leaves them out of words that have it; impossible to discover an American who considers a man who eats butter on his doughnuts to be reeking with prosperity; impossible to discover an American who believes his legs were made to stand upon.

In the meantime the great and amazingly durable vitality of Yankee character will have contributed no little toward forming the New American, the American who is slowly evolving from a melting pot that has seemed to melt too slowly but which in reality is melting as fast as it should. Synthesis of character requires longer cooking than does the making of plastic. That tough, resilient, cold-courage base in the New American—if he has one—that will have come in no small measure from Yankee influence.